Sterling Script

A Local Author Collection
2019

Walper Publishing
Sterling Heights, Michigan

Editors
Tuesday Morning Writers
Rena Davis, Zan Giese, Katy Hojnacki,
Terry Hojnacki, and Rebecca Eve Schweitzer

Editor-in-Chief
Terry Hojnacki

Cover Art & Design
Katy Hojnacki

ISBN: 978-1-949224-04-7
Volume Two of the Local Author Collection

The selections printed in this collection reflect the authors'
original work as submitted to the
Local Author Collection.

First Edition
1 2 3 4 5 6 7 8 9 10

Many thanks
to the authors and editors
in our vibrant writing community
for making this project possible –
a second time.

Happy Writing

TABLE of CONTENTS

Dear Reader,

Last year, the *Sterling Script* baby was born! Through community talent and support, I'm proud to share the toddler edition of *Sterling Script: A Local Author Collection.*

We continue our mission to support and encourage the local writing community by publishing their short stories, poetry, creative nonfiction works, and art. Whether you enjoy a fun-filled fantasy adventure, romantic poetry, or eerie tales, there is something for everyone in this collection.

As Nathaniel Hawthorne said, "Good reading is damn hard writing." Our authors have put in the hard work writing.

Happy Reading,

Terry

Sarah Lynne John

Sarah Lynne John fills her life checking off bucket list items, such as skydiving over Oahu, sampling escargot in Paris, cliff jumping in Utah, paragliding in the Alps, and even eating fruitcake in Siberia.

As a former communications professional, the power of the written word has always held a prominent place in her life. Now that her children leave for school each day, her passion is writing fiction. She relishes crafting stories that translate powerful emotions and share life's varied experiences.

Lily

Sarah Lynne John

Croquet hoops, balls and mallets scattered across the lawn forced me to choose my steps carefully. I had brought out Dean's old set after last night's family dinner. My grandkids loved it, and we hadn't bothered to tidy up. On the far side of the lawn, fragrant coral and white peony blossoms awaited my pruners. I heaved a sigh of relief and placed the heavy vases on the flower garden's small wrought iron table. The morning light sparkled on the dew, and my favorite family of robins chattered away in the nearby sycamore tree. I got to work harvesting newly opened blossoms, as well as buds the size and texture of marshmallows, in order to create two arrangements that would enjoy a long life. To this end, I placed the stems directly into tepid and slightly sweetened water in the vases.

Once satisfied with the aesthetics of the bouquets, I selected the largest and walked it over to my neighbor's. The door opened before I could knock.

"Good, I'm glad you saw me coming," I said, handing her the flowers.

She smiled and leaned into the bouquet, her beautiful face and clear blue eyes wreathed in petals. At 77, Beverly had twenty years on me, but she managed well despite being on her own.

"They smell divine," she said as she exhaled. "And what a

gorgeous bouquet! You've done it again. Thank you, Rachel!"

I just nodded and smiled. It felt good to have such an appreciative outlet for my hobby.

She went on, "I don't have a vase to return to you this week. I did what you said about trimming the stems every other day and replacing the water, and last week's tulip buds are open and thriving. You're going to run out of vases at this rate."

"Don't you worry about that. I have plenty. If you put them in the fridge at night, they'll last even longer."

"Oh, like a florist shop! I'll have to try that. Heaven knows there's plenty of space in there."

"Do you need me to run to the grocery for you?"

"No, no, bless your heart! You're too kind. Julia stocked me up this weekend. I meant that I don't require a fridge full of food anymore."

"Yes, I know what you mean. I'm glad your daughter helps out." My heart suddenly felt constricted as I thought of my own daughter.

~ ~ ~

There's nothing better after a morning of gardening than sitting to rest in front of fresh cut flowers with my herbal tea in a fine china teacup.

I drizzled a bit of honey in the tea and thought about my conversation with Beverly. Flowers tended to remind me of how fragile life is, especially cut flowers. First I grew and nurtured them from a seed, then, when they were young and starting to blossom, I separated them from their life-giving roots. I placed them in a brand-new environment and asked them to flourish. All my tricks to prolong their lives worked for a time, but in the end, they all died.

Well, that was a cheery thought. I opened my journal and flipped to the back where I had written my bucket list two years ago. At the time it seemed like a good, healthy technique. The purpose was to focus on what I could do with what was left of my life, rather than on what I had lost. So, I zip-lined, I parasailed, I visited the Statue of Liberty, and I witnessed a solar eclipse. One by one, I checked them off. Ride a camel and climb a pyramid in Egypt? Check. Learn to play chess? Check. I would say "check-mate," but I haven't been able to achieve that yet with my six-year-old grandson, Brandon. On a trip to Florida, I checked off two: I swam with a dolphin and wrote a poem for Evan, my child I lost stillbirth. I carved the poem with a piece of driftwood into the soft white sand of Siesta Key Beach. The rolling waves took the words into their arms one by one.

I never thought I would make it to the end of my list, but here I was, the last item.

- Make amends with Lily

There's no getting around it. Relationships are hard. Mother-daughter relationships are probably the most complicated. My own mother paid little attention to me. After my father left, her head was full of art and artists, especially the artists. I am certain my life amounted to a small checkbox item on her list. Give birth to a child. Check.

My pen hovered over the list. Maybe I should add more fun adventure items?

I conferred with Dean, my late husband. "What do you think, honey? Should I take that deep sea fishing trip you always wanted or set my sights on climbing the Eiffel Tower?"

I pictured him setting his thriller novel down in his lap and leaning back in his recliner. He'd know this was all bluster, that I wasn't in a position to travel. I could almost hear his response telling me to stop with the delay tactics, and how I would regret not getting my ducks in a row with Lily.

"Okay, okay," I replied, rolling my eyes and picking up my phone. I texted my youngest child, my baby, my only daughter. I asked her to meet me for lunch, my treat.

She declined. Said she was too busy. It didn't surprise me,

but it did feel as though she was wrenching my heart out with her bare hand like in *Indiana Jones and the Temple of Doom.*

I wondered if I could check it off now, or at least cross it out. I had tried, hadn't I? But I knew, without Dean raising his eyebrow at me, that it wasn't enough. I took a minute to ponder on what I could do to make things right between us.

With my first child, I swore I would not be like my mother. I know that's status quo, but it was her apathy that fueled my drive to be an engaged mother. And I was. With my sons, and then again with Lily. When she grew inside of me, and I felt her tiny body jump with hiccups again and again, I swore to help this girl of mine conquer the world.

Private schools, French lessons, ballet, violin, drama club, and ice skating—only the best of the best for my girl. Dean paid the bills and cheered her on, and bless him for that, but I was the one volunteering at school, screening her friends, persuading her to practice, shuttling her all over town, going to parent meetings, helping her study, sewing theater costumes, and bedazzling ice skating leotards for her competitions. Her acceptance to Columbia University was the pinnacle of my parenting career.

Somehow I needed to let go of the fact that she had thrown away my life's work, cast it off without a second glance in her second semester. Now she spent the day slapping sandwiches together at Subway. She shared a little apartment with roommates, and spent her time with a boyfriend who looked like he had several felonies under his belt. Thank heavens for my sons, or I would consider myself a complete failure.

I picked up the phone again, and before I could talk myself out of it, I dialed her number. She answered on the third ring.

"What is it, Mom? I'm headed to work."

Her tone was gruff and impatient. I tried to be rational. "Does a mother need a reason to call her daughter?"

"Can we do this later? Tom will let me have it if I don't

clock in on time."

"Okay, okay. Have a good day, sweetheart."

She grunted and hung up.

Tears pricked my eyes. I flicked my pen across the table. It fell on the floor.

Dean spoke up again from his chair assuring me that she'd come around, that I needed to keep trying.

I shot him a look and pushed away from the table. "Keep trying? Didn't you hear? She doesn't want anything to do with me!"

For the rest of the morning, despite an obnoxious headache, I busied myself with chores. It was Monday, laundry day. I turned up the radio and set about sorting my clothes, stripping the bed, and spot-treating the tablecloth from last night's dinner. What would it take for me to remember to avoid serving red sauces when my three grandchildren were present? Despite this, the familiar routines were soothing. When I tucked away my neatly folded underwear, my eyes came level with a photo on the bureau of us with Lily. She had her arms full of the roses we gave her after she starred in "Annie, Get Your Gun," and our arms were wrapped tight around her, full of love and parental pride.

I wondered where we had gone wrong. The radio blasted a Beatles song. I knew it, but this time the words jumped out at me like a flashing neon sign. It declared that life's too short for arguments.

Exactly the point, I thought. I listened to the rest of the lyrics. Over and over he asked his love to look at things from his perspective. He went on to explain that if she didn't, they wouldn't be able to work it out, and their love would be quits. That certainly wasn't an option for us. We were family. But, it hit me how I was guilty of the same egocentric approach to our situation. I felt sick to my stomach. Was the divide in our relationship my fault?

Well, I'm not one to sit around and stew on something. I

grabbed my keys.

~ ~ ~

It was lunchtime at Subway, and hungry customers formed a line to the counter. Lily had her hands full working the sandwich assembly and didn't see me come in. I stood there wondering what I could say. Gradually I found myself inching forward as more people came in behind me.

Her blue-green eyes met mine when my turn came. They pleaded with me to not make a scene. Before I could say anything, she asked which sandwich I wanted. I went down the line haphazardly selecting toppings, paid at the register and found a spot to sit. After a while I started nibbling on the sandwich. It turned out to be quite tasty and didn't take me long to finish. I played Scrabble on my phone while I waited. The customers tapered off as the afternoon wore on. I tried to think of a "q" word that didn't require a "u" when Lily plopped down in front of me, her Subway hat askew on her head and her arms folded across her chest.

"What is it that's so important you had to chase me down at work today? Is something wrong?"

For a minute I considered telling her. But it felt like cheating to tell her that the cancer was back. I didn't want her pity. I wanted her love.

"Mom, I have to get back to work."

"I...I just...I needed to see your face." I couldn't think what to say now that the moment had arrived. "We missed you at dinner again last night."

"Why? So you could berate me in front of the whole family, tell me again what a mess of things I've made?"

"No, of course not. I'm sorry. I want the best for you. I want you to be happy." Her hands were on the table now, and I took one. She let me; her hand lay like a limp noodle in mine.

Her eyes softened around the edges, but she continued to sit there in silence. I asked, "Are you happy working here?"

Immediately I regretted my words. Her face closed off

again. She pulled her hand away and stood up. "See, you just can't help yourself, can you? The judgement oozes out of you. Yes, I'm happy with my life right now. For the first time, I'm the one calling the shots, and I'm good with that. I'm sorry I'm not fulfilling your dreams for you. I'm sorry I'm not the daughter you always wanted." She started to walk away, then turned back, swiping away at her tears. "No, actually, I'm not sorry. I'm sorry my decisions hurt you, but I won't apologize for my choices. It's my life, and they're my choices."

She disappeared into the back before I could collect my thoughts.

Should I go over to the counter and call after her? No, I knew she wouldn't appreciate that.

I made it to the car before I began to cry. The tears turned to gut-wrenching sobs, and I started to hyperventilate. Was I having a panic attack? I couldn't breathe. My heart beat fast, and the sobs kept erupting. I knew I needed to calm down. Breathe in through the nose and out through the mouth, I coached myself. My heart started to settle, but my headache had grown to gigantic proportions. Despair overwhelmed me. What had I done wrong? It was clear that there wasn't going to be a reconciliation between us.

A frightening monster face looked back at me from the rearview mirror. Why had I put on mascara this morning? I wiped at it, but made it worse. I took another deep breath. Could this day get any more crummy? It had started out so serene and full of beauty.

By this time the lunch hour traffic had cleared, and it should have been an easy drive. The problem was that my vision began doing funny things—going blurry one minute, flashing with light and shadow the next. I thought I must have rubbed make-up into my eyes. I proceeded to head home at a snail's pace. My ten minute drive turned into thirty, but I made it. I collapsed back into my chair at the table. My face remained a mess, but I couldn't summon enough energy to go clean up. I was emotionally and physically exhausted. My journal sat there looking at me, daring me to confront my list. I flipped it open with the idea to cross out the last item and be done with it. But, no pen. Then I saw it on the floor across the room. It might as well have been across the Sahara desert.

The conversation with Lily replayed in my head. Well, I had wanted her point of view, and she'd given it to me. I looked at my list again. With a sudden burst of frustration, I tore the whole page from my journal, wadded it up and threw it in the trash.

I nearly jumped when I felt Dean's presence. He wrapped his arms around me, and a sort of calm flowed through my body. He reminded me that she was worth it, and that I didn't have much time.

As if on cue, my nose started to bleed—bright red splotches on my white linen blouse. I grabbed a fistful of tissues, but it kept bleeding, overflowing onto the floor. It dawned on me that this had passed the point of a normal nose bleed. I panicked. I've never liked the sight of blood, and it had dripped on everything. I grabbed a dish towel off the stove and mashed it against my face. A wave of dizziness swept over me. I clutched the kitchen island to keep from falling. My mind wouldn't focus. I didn't know what to do, so I waited. When the blood flow came to a stop, I cautiously made my way to my phone and called Andrew, my oldest.

He came right away and insisted on going to the hospital. They admitted me upon arrival. After a flurry of tests, the doctor gave me the news that the ovarian cancer recurrence had not responded well to the therapy, and in addition to this, it had metastasized to my brain and sinonasal cavity. He estimated that I would have two to three months to live without immediate surgery and radiation therapy.

I refused. I didn't want to go through another surgery. That was the plain and simple truth. I searched my mind for a reason to continue the fight, but I only found reasons to throw in my towel. My life had been a full one. Dean and Evan were waiting for me, I felt sure. I had finished all the things on my list that I could possibly do, hadn't I?

~ ~ ~

Andrew sat beside me in his wrinkled suit. His silence was a dead give-away. Most of the time he could talk your ear off, smooth as the salesman that he was. He hunched over his phone, avoiding my eye. His foot tapped incessantly. Yes, he was angry with me.

We had been in the hospital overnight and both our tempers were flaring. I hadn't changed my mind about the surgery, and he kept trying to shove the horrible hospital food down my throat. I had no appetite for it, no appetite at all, really.

His phone buzzed, and he looked like he'd been released from a starting gate. He rushed out the door, mumbling something about Jamison arriving.

It felt better without his additional angry energy in the room. I struggled to handle my own. I tried to relax into my pillow. They had given me something for the pain, but I hated that I had to be in the hospital. Every part of my body felt weighted down with fatigue, and I knew that I could look forward to another restless night full of unfamiliar noises and interruptions. Being tethered to an IV pole made me feel trapped and helpless. The one good thing was that they had cleaned the blood and mascara off my face.

My boys came into the hospital room. It cheered me up a bit to see them together. For two brothers who had teased each other mercilessly, they had turned out to be the best of friends.

Jamison, my middle child, must have done his thing, because Andrew looked much more at ease. He had always been the peacemaker in the family.

He took my hand with great care and sat on the edge of the bed. "Hi, Mom."

I soaked up the love I could see in his eyes and squeezed

his hand three times. This had always been our silent way of saying, "I love you."

He returned the message and continued, "We understand why you didn't want to tell us about the recurrence, and we can sympathize with why you don't want to fight it again. We know you love us and want to protect us."

A tear escaped and traced its way down my face. Jamison maintained perfect eye contact, and I found myself unable to look away.

He continued, "But the problem is that we want to be there for you, and we're not ready to say goodbye. You're young, Mom. There's a lot of life yet to be lived. Heaven can wait a little longer."

I opened my mouth to respond, but he stopped me by raising his hand. "No, Mom. You don't have to say anything right now. We respect your choice, and we will love you always whatever choice you make, but take some time to think about what I've said. Think about things from our perspective, and the perspective of your grandchildren who love you very much."

That afternoon while Jamison dozed in the chair beside me, I did think about his words. When had he become so wise? He was a counselor at the local high school, so maybe it came along with the job. I realized that however much I dreaded it, I needed to gear up for this battle, that I did want to use all the tools at hand to extend my life, whether it be months or years. I also now understood where I had gone wrong when it came to Lily.

The chance to tell her arrived sooner than I expected. She snuck into my room just half an hour later holding a large bouquet of lilies, my favorite. Jamison still slept. She set them on the table beside me.

For a moment I couldn't believe it was really her—that she cared enough to come for me. It brought fresh tears to my eyes. I didn't want to waste a single minute more of our lives with this problem between us. Grabbing hold of her arm like a lifeline, I jumped right in.

"Lily, I'm so glad you're here. Please forgive me. I realize now that I didn't respect your choices. I only saw how they reflected on me and my parenting. I want you to know that my love for you has never wavered. I'm ready to let you be responsible for your own choices and be your own person."

"Oh Mom," she said, her voice choked with emotion, "that's all I've wanted to hear. I love you, too."

She leaned over to hug me. We stayed that way long enough that I dozed off. When I woke she was gone. I assumed she needed to pull another shift at work. Jamison remained, working away on his laptop.

"I've decided to have the surgery," I told him.

"You will? Fantastic!" He gave me a quick hug and turned for the door. "I'll go tell the doctor."

"Jamison," I called before he could leave. "Did you get a chance to talk to Lily before she left?"

"Lily?"

"Yes, she stopped in while you were napping. She brought me these lilies." I pointed to the flowers next to the bed.

He looked stunned. "No, I didn't see her. I…I thought the nurse brought those in." He paused like he had more to say, but then changed his mind. "I'll be right back, Mom."

It seemed like quite some time before he came back, but he brought along a crowd of medical personnel. Over the flurry of activity that ensued he explained that an operating slot had opened up, and they were going to take me in now.

"I know it's a bit of a shock going straight into it like this," he began.

But I stopped him this time. "No, honey, it's a relief. I am ready no matter what the outcome is."

~ ~ ~

They put me under, and next thing I knew darkness enveloped me. A distant light came toward me, growing larger as it neared. It took the shape of a young man. A smile lit up his face, and recognition not born of my brain, but of

13

my heart, blazed through me. Could it be possible?

"Evan?" I asked.

He nodded and we embraced. When I pulled back to look at him again, Dean and Lily were there beside us, smiling as well. Dean appeared younger, like when we first met. He looked great, but I became too distracted and confused by Lily's presence to comment on it.

"Where am I?" I asked her. "I thought I was dying, but if that's the case, what are you doing here?"

She placed her hand on my shoulder. "I've been gone for two years. Remember, Mom? The car accident on campus?"

What could she be talking about? I tried to reason with her. "But, I talked to you. I saw you at work yesterday."

"Mom, I worked at the Subway on campus. It was my first job."

The memories flooded my mind in a rush. I felt the loss all over again, but tempered with the fact that she stood there before me, whole and beautiful.

I shook my head, trying to clear the confusion. "But it felt so real. How could this be?"

"You were suffering from a brain tumor, dear," Dean explained, "and a healthy dose of denial."

I couldn't believe it. How long had my mind been affected? How could I have believed these delusions were genuine? If I made it through this, I hoped the doctor would be able to get every bit of that tumor out of my head.

My daughter grasped both of my hands in hers. "I wanted to tell you I'm sorry. I'm sorry I went to that party. I shouldn't have gone in the car with those kids. I know my choices weren't the best."

I hugged her tight against me, and Dean and Evan wrapped their arms around us as well.

We had this brief moment together before Dean said that the time had come for me to go back, that it wasn't my turn yet. The love and joy from our happy reunion bubbled up inside of me. I wanted to stay forever, but I knew I had to return. Something had shifted inside me. I valued my life and would go on doing all I could to prolong it.

~ ~ ~

This time when I opened my eyes, Jamison stood beside me once again. He breathed a deep sigh of relief.

"What? You thought I wouldn't make it?" I joked. My voice came out weak and raspy.

"Well, you almost didn't." He held a cup of water with a straw to my mouth. "Your heart even stopped at one point during the surgery."

That makes sense, I thought.

"Everyone's in the waiting room, praying for you," he went on. "I should go let them know you made it through."

"Before you do, I need to tell you something." I patted the edge of the hospital bed. "Come, sit beside me for a minute while I tell you about the most amazing experience."

I couldn't have asked for a better listener. He didn't interrupt even when tears filled his eyes.

"I'm so relieved that you know about Lily," he said when I finished. "I thought it would be my job to break the news to you after recovery."

"There's something I don't understand." I looked over to make sure they were still there. "Who could have sent the lilies?"

He plucked the card out of the bouquet and read the words.

To a woman whose life is spent spreading sunshine and nourishment.
May you flourish where He plants you.
Love, Beverly

Michelle DeRoche

Michelle DeRoche is a lover of poetry and great stories, old and new. She believes herself to be more of a reader than a writer, but that does not mean her own tales aren't worth telling.

DeRoche is the proud holder of a Bachelor's Degree in English from the University of Detroit Mercy, where several of her original poems were published in the student arts journal, *[SIC]*. She is forever grateful she followed her literature-loving heart and stuck to her books, for they have carried her farther than she could ever imagine.

Trust Fall

Michelle DeRoche

There you were - a pillar -
A baffling rock - looming before me.

I stood away, looking up. Wondering. Afraid. Amazed.
Intrigued. A fearful, green explorer.
And you smiled.

Sweet. Warm. Coaxing.

I stepped towards you. Towards, what? But I went up.
Blindly
I shuffled - slow - around the winding path.
                        Inching along the unsteady ledge.
Curious and anxious.

Still you smiled. Warmer. You reached out and
                                    grasped my arm.
Up and up we wandered. I was uncertain, cautious.
But sure of you.

I slipped forward. Tripped.

You laughed. Pulled. Higher, now. I could feel the
                                  change in the air.
I closed my eyes, wandering around the next turn. Wondering
where we were.
Where your thoughts were.

You grew impatient.

Still, the curve of your lips drew us upward. Ever on.
It seemed an endless journey - a lifetime -
Lived within a mile.

I blinked. And there it was. The edge.

I looked down. Teetering. Shivering. With the whispers
Of the winds in my ears, I listened. I looked.
                              And I thought I saw you.
I closed my eyes.

I took a breath - I jumped - I fell.

I shattered.

Katy Hojnacki

Katy Hojnacki works with paintings, illustrations, novels, short stories, and even comics to delve into fantasy worlds. She is a writer, avid gamer, artist, and illustrator of the children's book *I Can See With My Eyes Shut Tight*. As cover designer and artist for *Sterling Script: A Local Author Collection*, she also contributes her writing and editorial skills to the publication.

A graduate of Oakland University with a degree in English and Studio Art, Hojnacki is an active member of the Sterling Heights Creative Writers Workshop as well as the Tuesday Morning Writers.

Tale of the Ferry

Katy Hojnacki

They say the best way for a curious child to adventure is to call the Ferry.

First, find a body of water. Any size will do, from a puddle to the sea. Behind my house, there's a river that churns brown in the summertime. Today, the darkened, pre-storm sky brought out the deep greens in the grass, trees, and the river water.

Second, write your name on a piece of paper, and fold it into a boat. I neatly scribed *Melody Reign* on a piece of sage-colored cardstock. As I put the cap on the permanent marker, it left a streak of green on my finger. The ink smeared off on the paper when I made my folds.

Third, the boat needs to hold two things: your favorite flower and a piece of fruit. The latter doesn't have to be your favorite, but it has to be a fruit. It's the only snack you're allowed. If you try to bring something that isn't a fruit or hide food, the Captain will be offended and not let you board - or worse.

A tiny paper boat can only hold so much, so I settled on four strawberries balanced in the corners of the craft. I laid my dandelion over the top.

Taking the boat in one hand and my shoes in the other, I crept down to the riverbank. My toes squished on my grassy perch. I stretched to set my boat into the water. The current swept up my paper vessel and hurried it to the main thoroughfare of the river.

Thunder rumbled above. I looked up to my house where the clouds were darkest. A drop of cool rain hit my arm, and I wondered if now might not be the best time to travel. Turning back to the river, I spotted my boat being lifted from the water by a giant, wooden oar.

The ferry was larger than I imagined.

The boat was long and thin, with half a dozen oars reaching into the river. Water glistened on the boat's sides, which were covered in giant, gleaming scales. The ferry's sides swelled as the scales shifted from shades of shimmering emerald green to the deep, mossy color of the river. A massive and detailed figurehead resembled the face of a dragon. Its eyes glowed a fiery red, and two trails of smoke drifted from its nostrils.

My boat slid down the arm of the Ferry's oar until snatched up by a tall man with spidery fingers. He examined my offering. As the oar dipped back into the water, he plucked the dandelion from the boat and sniffed it, then tapped each strawberry. He looked down to me. A chill ran through my back. My T-shirt was showing spots of rain as the wind kicked up.

"Melody," he said in the familiar musical way most people say my name, "would you like to come aboard?"

Fourth, when the Captain asks if you want to come on the ferry, do not say a word. All words spoken to the Captain can be used against you.

I nodded. It was hard to tear my eyes away from the ferry's scaled hull. It breathed.

The Captain whistled, and someone on the ship's deck ran over. After a few thuds, a long plank dropped from the ship and landed on the riverbank next to me, splattering mud on my ankles. I rinsed my feet in the water, clutched my shoes, and ran up the plank.

Once I was on the ship, the Captain turned and strode to

the back of the boat. My feet left a small puddle on the shiny, mahogany deck. Beside me, a boy who looked about my age heaved the gangplank back onto the boat. His skin was eerily pale and greenish.

"Hello," I said once he'd finished. The ferry lurched forward as the oars caught the water, then settled into the river's current. The sky continued to darken overhead.

The boy straightened and raised his hand to greet me. I flinched when he smiled; he had too many teeth, all of which were pointed and looked needle sharp. His face was narrow, and his ears came to knife-shaped peaks.

"I'm Melody," I said, trying to turn my stare into friendly eye contact. His eyes were a fierce gold, and his pupils thin like a cat's. "You?"

"Astra," he replied. "Was that where you were from? I haven't seen someone like you." He picked up a coil of silky rope and began walking to the front of the ship.

"Yeah." I followed him.

Astra stopped near a large winch. As he cranked the handle, the rope slithered into coils around the device.

My feet had stopped leaving drips behind on the warm deck, so I slipped my shoes on. "Where are *you* from?"

"Somewhere brighter," he said. He paused to look off the ship, so I looked, too.

The sky had darkened to a deep purple. The river swirled thick and black. It widened; the distant coasts were speckled with red veins. I leaned over the railing and watched the water gurgle. A bubble popped and spat drops onto the side of the boat, leaving inky trails behind them.

"Whoa," I said, stepping back from the railing.

Astra laughed. "You get used to it."

"How can you get used to something like *this*?" I asked as I watched something slimy and dark slip above the water. The thick river completely obscured whatever creature it might belong to. Squinting, I leaned over and gripped the railing with sweating palms.

"I've been here a long time," said Astra, abandoning the winch handle and looking over the edge of the boat with me.

"I've never seen anything like it," I said. This gross river and strange sky were way cooler than any adventure I might have imagined.

I sprang back from the railing. Something slick and solid, like weird, warm bugs crawled between my fingers. I opened my hands and saw several shimmering marbles materializing from nothing, collecting in my palms. They radiated a faint, orange light.

"Marvelous, Melody," said the Captain from over my shoulder.

Astra didn't flinch, but I did. I bit my lip, remembering the fourth rule.

"I expected something more…golden, but these will do," continued the Captain. He reached one of his long arms over me and prodded at the orbs. Satisfied, he turned and said, "Astra?"

Astra nodded and nudged my arm. I glanced between him and my new collection, still cupped in my hands. He gestured for me to follow him, and we proceeded toward the stairs in the center of the ship while the Captain returned to his place at the rear of the boat.

"What the heck are these things?" I hissed at Astra as soon as I thought the Captain was out of earshot. The little orbs grew uncomfortably warm.

"It happens while you're here," he said, shrugging as he descended the stairs. They creaked under his feet. "Whenever it does, hold onto them and come down here to drop them in the Belly."

I cradled my hands close to my chest while climbing down the stairs. Below deck, the room was spacious. The same polished mahogany as above deck made up the walls, floor, and ceiling. Several empty benches lined the walls, and the oar handles poking through the hull appeared to be rowing of their own accord.

In the center of the room, a shiny, black stove crackled. A fiery glow peeked through the gaps of a small door on the side of the device. The stove's lopsided shape reminded me of a bean. Several people were gathered around it, looking as strange or stranger than Astra.

Swinging his arm toward the stove, Astra announced half-heartedly, "The Belly of the Dragon." At the sound of his voice, everyone turned to look at us. One was shorter than me, with silvery scales instead of skin and long, grey fins draping his face. Another was only vaguely human-shaped and more closely resembled blue raspberry Jell-O than a person.

"Someone new, Astra?" said a high, sing-songy voice. A tall, lean looking girl with mossy hair stepped away from the group. Her skin was deep brown and textured like tree bark.

"Step aside, she needs to load the Belly," said Astra, waving the girl away. Everyone stepped back for me to approach the furnace. Astra picked up a fire poker from next to the Belly, hooked it onto the furnace door, and yanked the stove open. A rush of heat hit my face from a large pile of fiery, glowing orbs inside.

Clutching my hands together to be sure no marbles escaped, I tossed them into the furnace. They hissed when they hit the pile. The ship rumbled, and a low, throaty growl filled the room. Astra slammed the furnace shut, and I wiped my hands on my jean shorts.

"Guess you're good enough for the Dragon," said Astra, tossing the poker down. He turned to the group. "Everyone, this is Melody. She's from Grey-Sky-Green-River."

"Michigan," I corrected him.

"Grey-Sky-Green-River is apparently called Mish Again," said Astra. He bit his lip to restrain a frown, and I saw a flash of his needle-like teeth. The group remained silent for a moment.

"I am called Fern," said the tall girl warmly. She stepped back to allow me space in their conversation circle. "I am also from a Green-River place." She seemed to struggle with the words, like they didn't fit in her mouth. Gracefully, she gestured to the others. Flecks of light blue lichen decorated her twiggy fingers. "They are called Hydri and Zug."

Zug, the slimy looking one, gurgled at me. The fin on top of Hydri's head flicked open and closed, revealing a bright red interior. I decided this was a wave, so I waved back.

"Nice to meet you, Fern," I said. "And you, too, Hydri and Zug."

"I should get back on deck," said Astra. He was already heading toward the stairs.

"Astra's always busy," said Hydri, glaring after Astra. A forked tongue stuck out of the fish person's mouth. "Captain's favorite."

"You can come help me instead of talking about me behind my back," said Astra without turning around. Hydri let out a bubbly laugh, then ran after Astra. Hydri's finned feet slapped on the wood floor.

"So you're from a place with a green river?" I tilted my head up at Fern. "What's it called?"

"We do not share the names of our homes," said Fern. Her hands moved stiffly as she spoke. She smelled like a garden in the summertime. "Astra says it is…confusing. It is easier to recognize when someone will go home by the colors. I am from Black-Sky-Green-River."

"Sounds dark," I said. "Is it scary?" I glanced at Zug, but Zug seemed to be perfectly content listening.

"No, it is not scary," said Fern. "It is…beautiful, and safe, and deep. There are people and very tall plants who look like me."

"Trees?" I provided. "I love trees."

"Trees," said Fern fondly, her smile somehow touching

her solid black eyes. "Yes. Very big ones."

"That sounds nice," I said, but a shout from on deck interrupted us. Fern, Zug, and I all looked to the hatch leading to the deck.

"FERN!" shouted Hydri. "Black-Sky-Green-River!"

Fern's face folded into a wide smile. Small beads of golden tears formed at the corners of her eyes. She ran for the stairs.

Zug and I followed. When I noticed that Zug left a trail of aqua slime with each step, I quickened my pace to reach the ladder first.

The sky was dark, but only because the largest trees I had ever seen stretched for miles into the air. Their thick leaves and heavy branches blocked out any light from the sun - was there a sun here? Patches of glowing, blue mushrooms illuminated the forest. The mushrooms grew on the ground, on the tree trunks, and even at the bottom of the river, where they appeared green. The air felt heavy, but warm.

"It's beautiful," I said. Hydri leaned dangerously far over the railing. A few tiny yellow beads fell from Zug's hands like raindrops. Astra's expression was flat and hard to read. I cast him a curious look, but he turned his attention to the river.

"Home," Fern said. The patches of lichen on her body glowed the same shade of blue as the forest. Tears streamed from her eyes. They fell and collected on the deck. I noticed they were not tears but more glowing, golden orbs for the furnace below.

I had not noticed the Captain come up behind Fern. His pale, spidery fingers wandered up her back. Fern's tears began to trail backwards, drawn to the Captain's hand. They gathered into a large, glowing ball. Fern gasped and turned slowly to see the Captain. A smirk crawled across his gaunt face.

A tremendous crack echoed through the forest, like a tree splitting from lightning.

A glowing fissure coursed through Fern, cleaving her in

half. Thousands of gold orbs burst from the gap. The flow pulsed and gushed from the wound. Most rushed to the Captain, but some lost marbles scattered across the ferry's deck.

A pile of golden orbs remained where Fern once stood.

My fingernails bit into my hands. I glared at the Captain, my insides cradling a sparking swell of rage.

"How *dare* you! You killed her!" The words escaped before I could hold them back. "How could you? She was *home!*"

Before, the Captain did not stand out to me. Compared to the odd sights and people on the ship, he seemed normal. As his fingers twiddled with excitement, I watched the lines disappear from his face. He loomed over me, unusually tall. Even his clothing seemed more vibrant. The emerald green of his vest and pants sparkled with the faint light from the pile of golden orbs at his feet. He glistened, bright as the scales on the hull of his Ferry.

A smile curled his mouth and revealed sharp, black teeth. Shimmering goo dribbled from his thin lips. A drip stretched and splattered on the deck, matching Fern's remains.

Regret dropped in my stomach like a rock in the river.

I stepped back slowly. Tearing my eyes from the Captain, I met Astra's gaze. His almond eyes were wide, but I couldn't read his expression. Hydri was comforting Zug, who made a despondent-sounding gurgle. The Captain's eyes dug into me. Steeling my expression, I met his gaze again.

Grin still plastered on his face, the Captain broke into an eerie laugh. It carried through the trees like a cicada's scream. When he stopped, his eyes swept over the gold orbs scattered across the deck.

"Go load the Belly," said the Captain, tone both jovial and cruel. He let out a deep sigh as he sauntered to the back of the boat.

Astra moved first. Opening a chest on the far side of the boat, he pulled out a pair of shovels and a stack of pails.

Hydri tugged at Zug. Zug stared at the largest pile of golden marbles and appeared to be melting a little. The mahogany deck darkened with a blue tinge. Astra cast everyone a warning look before he scooped up the rogue balls with a shovel, dumping them into a pail. Silent and shaky, we cleaned.

Once we transported the filled pails below deck, we stood in front of the Belly of the Dragon. Astra made no ceremony of hurling the contents into the furnace. The furnace sizzled with a renewed fervor. Astra slammed the door shut with a bang.

"I'm an idiot," I said. My hands clawed at my hair. "I can't believe I said that. Said *anything*. I know the rules. I'm so stupid."

"It happens," said Astra. He stacked the pails and folded his light green arms. "It's the same thing every time." Astra maintained a matter-of-fact tone. "They travel, they see amazing places, they get homesick. Right when he thinks they've given up hope to see home again, he takes them there. It's the most... productive."

Hydri fidgeted with his head fins. Zug shrank from a human shape to a glob close to the floor.

"Best to accept it now," said Astra. "It's how they all go." His gaze flicked up to me. "Except Melody. She'll get worse."

"Worse?" My hands tangled in my hair at my temples. "What's worse?"

Astra shrugged. "I haven't seen anyone stupid enough to call the Captain out. It'll be a learning experience for everyone." Sighing, he picked up the stack of pails and walked away from the furnace. "I know we all liked Fern, but take my advice. It's better not to get attached to anyone here."

I huffed and raced after Astra.

"If you've been here so long, why don't you do anything about it?" I said, blocking his way to the stairs. "How come

29

the Captain hasn't gotten rid of *you* and sent *you* home yet?"

Astra stopped before he ran into me. A flicker of annoyance disrupted his neutral expression.

"Have you had anything to eat yet, Melody?"

"Answer my question!" My stomach growled anyway at the mention of food.

"You brought the red ones, right?" said Astra, gesturing for me to go up the stairs. The gesture evolved to a gentle shove when I wouldn't move, so I glowered at him before complying.

I scanned the empty deck. "Where's the Captain?"

Astra didn't answer, but I saw his gaze dart side to side before he walked to the back of the ship. I followed him, looking to the horizon.

We were no longer in Black-Sky-Green-River. The swirling, grey sky loomed overhead. Dark creatures flew in circles around jagged, black peaks in the distance. The river flowed thick and milky white around the Ferry. The place reminded me of winter back home, but the air was comfortable, not bitter cold. Curious, I squinted into the distance to identify the flying creatures.

I felt the orange marbles forming in my palms and tore my eyes away. I glared at the small orbs before hurling them into the ivory water. They made the soft plunks of failed skipping stones.

"*Melody*," Astra corrected me without looking. He stopped in front of a large, wooden chest and jammed a key into the lock.

"No," I snapped as he creaked the chest open. "You need to start answering questions, Astra."

"Are these you?" said Astra, holding up my four strawberries.

"Yes, but that's not the point!" I snatched the strawberries from his hand. My stomach longed for food, and the dark red fruits looked delicious. I bit into one and nibbled around the stem to get as much of the fruit as I could. The perfect berry filled my mouth with juicy sweetness.

The chest slammed shut. Astra straightened and leaned on it, watching me as I picked the strawberry's stem clean. My sudden hunger and anger melted away with each berry. When I'd finished, my stomach was stuffed.

"The Captain hasn't gotten rid of me because I don't miss home," said Astra. "There's nothing to gain from me except that I keep everyone else in line. Mostly, he doesn't know what to do with me."

I frowned, fidgeting with the leftover strawberry stems.

"I can't help anyone, because then he might decide otherwise," Astra continued, folding his arms. With our surroundings so grey, his green skin looked vivid and alien. "So I do my part and keep the ship running smoothly, because I don't want to find out what the Captain would do if I don't."

"Well, I don't want to find out how he's going to deal with me," I said, flicking the strawberry stems off the ship. "So we should do something about it."

"Why? You came here for an adventure, didn't you?" said Astra, turning his gold eyes on me. "Were you expecting one without consequences? Let me guess, you want to rally everyone here, overwhelm the Captain, take over the ship, and get everyone home safely?"

"Well—" I began. My shoulders shrank. "I mean, it'd work, wouldn't it?"

"You *are* an idiot," said Astra, his nose scrunching. "That's a great way to become food for the Belly. Unless you're more dangerous than you look, the Captain will turn you into a smear on the deck without even dirtying a finger."

"Even if it doesn't work, at least I'd be *doing* something," I snapped at Astra. "What happened to Fern isn't happening again. I'll make sure of it, one way or another."

Scoffing, Astra turned his attention to a cloud of silvery

insects hovering near the railing. The little bugs were making quick work of building a nest on the wood; in seconds they wove a lacey web. I turned away before the creatures stole my interest any further.

"I'm going to talk to the others," I said.

"I think Zug's next," said Astra, swatting at the bugs. His finger tore through their silky fibers. "Behind quota."

Huffing, I spun on my heel to leave Astra to his pest control. I froze when I saw the Captain striding in our direction. His pointed nose turned to the grey sky, and he took a breath of the warm air.

"All hands on deck," he called. His voice carried as far as it needed to without having to escalate to a yell.

Astra gave the railing a last brush with his hand before standing tall, facing the Captain. I mirrored Astra as Hydri and Zug scrambled on deck. Zug still looked exceptionally sludgy, and only stretched as tall as Hydri's hip.

"We'll be docking shortly." The Captain's gaze stayed on the horizon even while he addressed us. Our vessel had turned to face one of the enormous ebony mountains. "The Ferry's grown dirty. Zug, Hydri, I need you scrubbing her clean as soon as we stop. Zug on port, Hydri on starboard. Melody, I need you preparing our lines, relaxing the keel, securing the Belly of the Dragon, tying us off, and adding fertilizer as well as the most recent flower to the Vagabond's Garden."

I tried to decode the Captain's instructions. In all the sailing stories I'd read, the ships had sails, not furnaces, and none of them breathed like a dragon. Where was I supposed to start? Hydri and Zug exchanged a look before their eyes fell on Astra, who stood behind me.

I turned. Astra opened his mouth and shut it again. His teeth dug into his lip, and his fingers twitched at his sides.

"And..." The Captain's gaze wandered the ivory waves off-ship before settling on Astra. A smile curled on his face.

"Oh, of course. You… make sure she knows how to do that, yes? Crew dismissed."

Astra rushed past me. He kept his voice low, but the cutting tone remained intact as he spat my name. "Melody. Follow me."

I chased Astra as he headed below deck. Paying no attention to whether or not I could keep up, he turned and opened a door I never noticed near the base of the stairs. We squeezed through a short hallway to a supply closet. Stacks of buckets rolled back and forth on the floor between spaghetti noodle piles of silken rope.

Astra quickly demonstrated how to coil rope. He twisted his wrist while making the loops so that it would not twirl together. Demonstration complete, he shut me into the closet and left me to straighten the room. My thoughts raced with the long list of tasks from the Captain, so I grabbed some rope and got to work.

A room of rope later, Astra returned, as though he knew when I would finish.

Before I could even say hello, Astra said, "Grab a few buckets." He slid past me and moved aside a few mops propped against another door.

"Where are we headed now?" I said, scooping up a stack of buckets and tucking them under my arm.

Astra said nothing as we proceeded down a long hallway. After walking the deck of the ship several times, I was pretty sure this hallway was longer than the ship itself. It seemed to be curving slightly, and I felt dizzy with an elevation change I could sense, but not see.

The hall opened into a room where the walls were lined with pulsating vats. They were the size of the boiler in my basement back home, but filled with a golden goo. Astra and I slipped behind the tubes, where several buckets collected drips. We swapped out the buckets for empty ones.

"What is this stuff?" I looked closely as it sloshed in the

bucket. I saw the top of Astra's spiky haired head drop through a door in the floor. Sighing, I lined my feet up with the short ladder and descended after him.

The floor crunched when I stepped on it. Spooked, I stepped back up the ladder. Dull, brittle looking scales from the Ferry's exterior hull covered the floor. A bulky, tarnished lock sealed the only other door in the room.

"Watch it," said Astra, shuffling through the scales. He set the buckets down and impatiently waved for me to get off the ladder.

I slid my feet in under the scales to find the wooden floor beneath and rested the buckets on the scales. Astra threw a brush at my chest.

"Scrub the scales with *that*," he said, nodding to the buckets of golden goo, "until they're shiny." He provided no other commentary before shoving me aside and disappearing up the ladder.

As I polished the scales, all I could think about was Fern, the Captain, and how I needed to get us off this ferry safely. And how Astra wouldn't talk to me except to tell me what to do. It felt like ages since I had spoken to the others.

I sat in a pile of shined, emerald scales when I heard Astra's footsteps overhead. The skin on my hands peeled, and the golden goo left stains on my jean shorts. He dropped down, pulled a key from a pouch on his hip, and unlocked the door. We entered yet another room too big for the ship.

The floor had a large, rectangular gap. Underneath it, a bed of green scales rose and fell. I could see patches of soft, yellow flesh between the scales. Hypnotized by the breathing hull, I had forgotten my complaints for Astra.

"Fill in the gaps and smooth it over with that mop." Astra's voice echoed from the scale room.

After what must have been hours of struggling with the bouncy hull and the awkwardly large mop, I clambored back to the scale room to find Astra waiting.

"Vagabond's Garden. Come on," he said. I scrambled to my feet and followed him up the ladder before he slammed the trap door shut. Despite Astra's hurried pace, I stayed close behind him. Remembering our path was a lost cause. I chewed my tongue as I tried to come up with what to say.

Our latest excursion led to a room with a low ceiling, though it was about the same size as the primary room below-deck, where the Belly and moving oars could be found. A gold glow filled the room thanks to goo-filled tubes lining the ceiling. The floor was covered in rich, black soil. The hundreds of bizarre, colorful flowers poking out of the dirt smelled like the muck on a soccer field.

Astra wove his way between the larger plants to a shelf at the back of the room, where five pots held a few tiny flowers. I spotted my dandelion.

Astra pulled one of the pots out and shoved it at me. I caught it before he let go. The flower inside had wide, stiff petals that crinkled like a strange mushroom. I recognized the color as the pale, glowing blue of the fungi from Black-Sky-Green-River. I bit my lip.

"Is this—?"

"Who else's would it be?" Astra said, taking careful footsteps around the plants. He found a gap between them and carved a divot in the dirt with his toes. "It has to go here."

"How is everyone? Have we landed yet?" I said, being extra careful not to crunch any plants as I joined Astra in the midst of the garden.

"Keep the pot. It's part of the fertilizer."

"You are the *worst* at answering questions," I said, stopping next to a spiky, red plant with delicate white flowers.

"Don't waste time, Melody." Astra rolled his eyes and waved me over.

"Why are you all mad at me?"

"Can we just put the stupid plant in the stupid garden?"

said Astra, slashing his hand at the dirt-covered floor. "Haven't you done enough?"

"No, I haven't done enough," I snapped. My shaking hands clawed into the pot I held. "Not while people like Fern—"

"—The *plant*, Melody." Astra sighed and held out his hand.

"How many of these plants were brought by people you knew?" The clay walls of the pot cracked under my fingers, and grainy dirt trickled through. "How many more spots are we going to dig?"

Growling, Astra took a swift step toward me. I tried to lean away from him, but he ripped the pot out of my hands. Returning to the divot in the dirt, he crouched and crumbled the pot and its contents into the space. He swept up the soil and mounded it around Fern's flower. The mushroom-like blossom looked small compared to the others here in the Vagabond's Garden.

I seethed, biting my tongue. His pale green hands interacted with the soil so gently, and the kindness he showed to the plant melted my anger for moment.

"We need to go back on deck," said Astra, standing.

We moved briskly back through the labyrinthian ship. I was not entirely positive how to navigate the vessel anymore, so I followed Astra. Which Sky and River place was it now? How long had it been since I'd been above deck?

The dreariness of Grey-Sky-White-River greeted us outside. The milky river lapped against the Ferry's hull, and the sky was a deeper grey than I remembered. A few golden lanterns created pockets of warm light around the deck, but Astra and I seemed to be alone as he led us to the ship's stern. I waited, watching the distant, dark mountains while he fumbled with a pile of ropes and tools.

Astra cleared his throat.

I turned my attention back to him and flinched. He had an

unexpectedly long, shimmering knife pointed at me.

"Whoa, what are you doing?" I said, holding my hands up defensively.

"Sorry, Melody," said Astra. I didn't hear an ounce of regret in his voice as he approached me. "I can't let you stay on this ship."

"What are you talking about?" The blade reflected the dark grey sky. "Astra, don't."

"I know the patterns, okay?" said Astra, jabbing the knife toward me, but it was a threat, not an attack. "The Captain's phasing me out. I can't let that happen. And if you're still here when we land, I'm useless."

"Don't say that, Astra, we can work together!" I recoiled until my back brushed the railing. "You don't have to do this."

"Melody, I have *one* job here—keep things in order. And you've messed up all of it. This is the only thing I *can* do. So, are you going to make this easy or difficult?"

I pushed off from the railing and charged him. Astra's eyes went wide. He meekly held out the knife, but I shoved his arm aside before we both fell to the deck. Astra squirmed to get the blade between us. I dug my knee into his chest, gaining leverage so I could pin down his wrist and yank the knife from it.

My heart pounded in my ears. Knife in hand, I leaned back from Astra and was about to get to my feet when I heard wet, sloppy footsteps. Hydri and Zug both ran across the deck toward us.

"ASTRA!" yelled Hydri.

Fins flapping, Hydri reached us when I disentangled from Astra. I stumbled to my feet. Astra scooted nearer to Zug, who had stopped abruptly with a squelching sound. The deck's golden lanterns shimmered through Zug's jelly body and glinted on Astra's stern gaze.

"Don't you *touch* Astra," said Hydri, wedging himself

between Astra and me.

My words froze in my throat. I hadn't started this. Astra had. But with the knife in my hand, they wouldn't believe me.

Hydri held up his fists. Two sharp, red fins extended from his forearms with a snap. Hydri advanced, slashing his new fins at me. I backpedaled, only bringing the knife up to deflect a strike I could not avoid. The blade caught on a spine in Hydri's left fin. I felt the handle slipping from my already sweaty hands, and the weapon flung across the deck.

The knife skidded until it came to a stop against the Captain's boot.

"My, my, is there a problem here?" said the Captain. His black eyes drifted from me, to Hydri, to Zug, and lastly to Astra. We exchanged no glances and said no words.

The Captain let out a sigh that seemed to carry a breeze across the entire ship. The lanterns bobbed in time with his steps as he sauntered to the rear of the ship.

"No explanation?" said the Captain. "Astra, do fetch a mop."

A whistle in the wind caught my attention. Zug stretched taller, and the fins on Hydri's head flipped up. I found my mouth watering with the sweet sensation of strawberries. The sound manifested into a lilting melody, and I realized it was coming from the Captain.

My body relaxed, and my limbs became heavy. Zug and Hydri swayed with me to the song. The music carried on even as the Captain chuckled softly.

"Melody Reign," he said. When he opened his mouth to speak again, the sound was jarring—it was *my* voice. "*How dare you*—" shouted my own fevered cry. Then, ripped out of context, "*Kill—Her.*"

Zug's sludgy body quivered and swelled into a massive blob. It throbbed and lurched toward me. Hydri turned, poised to attack with his forearm fins.

I could not move. I tried to speak, but my mouth was

clogged with juicy strawberries. I didn't just taste them. Sweet mush formed firm berries until I could feel their tiny seed bumps on my tongue.

Zug and Hydri collided on their way to get to me. They glared at each other, seeming to forget about me in their frenzy. Zug's swollen body mashed into Hydri, who slashed defensively. A stream of golden orbs slick with bluish sludge burst from Zug, spilling across the deck. Hydri lost his footing as he tried to scramble over them. Zug surged and slammed over Hydri with a wet slap. I winced as I saw the shadow of Hydri's struggling form under Zug.

No, no, no! The blue liquid from Zug leached through my shoes and soaked my toes, but I still could not move or speak. With great effort I turned my eyes to the Captain. He turned his back to us, content to let the brutality play out.

Astra followed behind the Captain. I spotted the blade back in his hand as he quickly wound a length of twine around the knife's handle.

I was furious with Astra. Hydri and Zug didn't want to hurt me. But Astra was letting this happen like he let every other awful thing happen on the Ferry. My anger surged, but the spell didn't break.

Astra plunged the knife into the Captain's back. Screams filled the air—not the Captain's or Astra's, but dozens of voices lifting a war cry together. The Captain reeled. His long fingers stretched into golden claws, and he swatted at Astra. The boy ducked, darting behind the Captain and yanking the knife out.

They clashed. The Captain hissed like water on coals. His metallic hands shed no blood from the blade's scratches. With each slash, Astra's knife screamed. I recognized a voice among them—*Fern.*

I opened my mouth and spat out the strawberries. As I sputtered the last of their juices onto the deck, my legs loosened. I staggered back from Hydri and Zug; Hydri was still trapped, motionless beneath Zug's enormous body. My muscles quivered, anxious to hit something or sprint. My feet pounded the deck as I ran at Astra and the Captain.

The Captain's claw hooked Astra's shoulder. The knife slipped from Astra's hand and clunked on the mahogany deck. Astra dangled as the Captain lifted his catch, surveying the boy as he might a boot dredged up while fishing.

"Mutiny," spat the Captain.

I grabbed the knife. Astra had wrapped leaves and sprigs from the Vagabond's Garden around the handle. They whispered in languages I didn't know, mother tongues from lands only the Ferry's river touched. They longed for the Captain.

I tore the plants from their ties and charged the Captain. He shook Astra from his claw and slashed at my back and shoulder as I shoved my fist full of flowers into his wound. The whispers turned to shouts as the captain doubled over.

Astra rolled and rose to his feet. Even as blood gushed from his shoulder, his expression was livid. Shoving me back, he ripped the knife away and jammed it back into the Captain's wound.

The wound shot out golden rays of light, brightening the deck as though the sun was rising over the river.

I threw my arms up to cover my eyes. The light coalesced into the familiar golden marbles, like when the Captain attacked Fern, but now the tiny orbs flooded from the Captain into *Astra*. His body reeled as though in pain. He abandoned the knife and clutched his chest.

The Captain's face thinned before my eyes. His skin paled and stuck to his brittle cheekbones. His eyes and mouth dribbled gold, and the viscous stuff sizzled on the deck as it puddled at our feet.

The knife dropped. The Captain disappeared into a wisp of green smoke. A pile of glistening, emerald bones landed on the deck, clattering like broken glass.

Behind me, Astra's skin glowed. Gold dripped from his eyes, his mouth, his hands. The shimmering liquid rolled over his shoulder, sealing his earlier wound. His shallow, irregular breathing and distant stare set my nerves on edge.

"Astra?" I asked tentatively. The back of my T-shirt grew warmer and wetter with each of my racing heartbeats. The Captain had cut me. It didn't hurt. Just wet, pulsing, exposed. "What did you do?"

Astra dropped to his knees, bracing himself on the deck. He wiped the liquid from his mouth, sending a glistening drop racing past his wrist and down to his elbow.

"I ended it."

But it wasn't over. Zug still throbbed on the deck. Straightening, Astra shoved me away, smearing some of the gold on my back. I shuddered as my skin tightened and fused back together. He surveyed the scene with a look of mild disgust more befitting of the late Captain, until clarity flashed in his golden eyes.

"Hydri," he gasped. He pushed at Zug's sturdy mass, and Zug began to shrivel, flopping easily away from the fish person underneath. Zug reformed to normal size, shuddered, and let out a whimper.

Hydri did not move. He lay on the deck, heavy and limp; his eyes were open, but empty. When Astra's finger brushed up against Hydri's scales, several of them chipped and flaked off. Astra's distant look returned.

"Get your flower, Melody," said Astra coldly. "We're taking you home first."

~ ~ ~

As we traveled from river to river, I stared into the sunshiny bloom of my dandelion. Somehow, the blossom never closed like the other dandelions I had picked, despite how long it had been since I plucked the flower. I couldn't get Hydri's image out of my head until my flower started spitting tiny gold embers. They floated up toward a familiar blue sky. Fiery orange leaves fluttered over the river.

Yellow marbles filled my palms. I scraped them into the pot and called, "We're here."

"This is Blue-Sky-Brown-River," said Astra.

"No. This is my home," I said, showing him the orbs in the pot. I wanted to be excited—I knew my river, but something felt wrong. I could see my house further up on the banks. Black trash bags were piled against the side of the garage.

Astra frowned at it, but seemed to find it suitable evidence. He whistled for Zug.

"Where I'm from, skies and rivers change," I said. "I'm sorry."

"You wanted an adventure, didn't you?" said Astra, dragging the gangplank over with Zug's help. They shoved the slimed side off the boat, where it smacked on the riverbank.

"At least you have a home now," I said, stepping onto the plank.

Astra paused before waving me off the boat. "If I had let you kill him, it would have been yours."

~ ~ ~

The busy lunchroom buzzed around me. Dozens of conversations overlapped each other. I kept my face buried in my chemistry workbook, as I had for the last several days during lunch.

Chelsea fluffed my hair before slamming her books down on the table next to me. I flinched at the sound, sighing as she started to unpack her lunch. Avoiding my friends was tougher than the homework.

"Chels, please," I said. "I still have 12 pages left to catch up."

"You tried it, didn't you?" she said, brushing dark curls from her face so she could crunch into a baby carrot.

"Tried what."

"*The ritual*," she said. "That's why you were gone? You were on the news. My mom thought you got kidnapped by human traffickers. But it was the Ferry, wasn't it?"

My parents sobbed when I had come home. My mother wouldn't stop touching the blood stains on the back of my T-shirt while my father dialed the police to update my missing person's case. Before long, the police showed up, demanding to know where I had been. Asking who took me, what they looked like, how they hurt me.

"No," I said.

I pictured Fern's back cleaving in half, spilling golden orbs all over the Ferry's deck. The Captain's eerie, cicada-scream laugh. Astra wiping sticky, blue slime from Hydri's limp body. Astra's horrified expression as those same marbles expelled from Hydri's mouth like a last breath. Zug's haunting whines.

"I ran away from home." My reply was robotic. "I don't want to talk about it."

Fifth: Tell no one about the Ferry.

a tint of rain

Artist: Katy Hojnacki

Rebecca Eve Schweitzer

Rebecca Eve Schweitzer is a writer, artist, editor, social media consultant, marketer, zine maker and word nerd based in Metro-Detroit. She has an overactive imagination, hordes books like a dragon, and would like to be a unicorn or phoenix should she ever be forced to grow up.

She is a member of the Sterling Script editorial board, a founding member of the Tuesday Morning Writers, and an active participant of the Sterling Heights Creative Writing Workshop. Her writing, art, zines, and blog can be found at www.beccaeve.com.

Casual Funeral

Rebecca Eve Schweitzer

You're invited!
Please join us to celebrate the life of Gary Lynn Hamstead
Where: Gary's house! (Stay out of Carol's house!)
When: March 23, noon
Who: You, silly!
Light snack-ish foods will be served (BYOB)
Business casual attire required

The invitation would be a mess. Carol had not been able to convince Gary that funeral invitations weren't really a thing, especially when those invitations had dancing dinosaurs on them. He had insisted though. He had also insisted on that exact text. He thought the business casual line was hilarious.

Gary had planned his funeral countless times. He had changed it so much Carol would have to check all of his paperwork and devices to make sure there wasn't something even newer. She always thought she'd ignore what Gary wanted and do the normal funeral set-up, but when the police arrived at her house to tell her that Gary had died, his endless babble about his funeral arrangements broke through her gasping and made her start laughing.

The police did not know what to do.

Carol did not live with Gary, but the married couple was

very much in love. Two separate houses on the same block just seemed more convenient to both of them. The backyards connected. They had a little gate they could pass through. After an incident of unintentional streaking about 15 years ago, Gary had put up a privacy fence pathway that ran along one side of both yards near their back doors. He also put up a privacy fence at the far end of the yards, since the single-sided fence felt off. They had their own little compound.

When Carol started laughing hysterically, the police asked if there was anyone they could call. Carol tried to compose herself, sure the police were about to call for some sort of mental health professional, but it just made her laugh harder remembering Gary's request to be buried in a straight jacket.

One police officer approached her with a real estate agent magnet that Gary had labeled "Carol's mother. Emergency use only."

"Is this your mother? May we contact her?" asked the other officer.

Carol nodded through her laughter. She didn't have anyone else to call.

"Is this the best number?" he asked, holding up the magnet for her to see.

Carol nodded again. Her mother's business phone number was the only number Carol had for her. The woman was all business. Her mother hated Gary. She'll probably be thrilled to have him gone.

To Carol's surprise, the police—one had said he was a detective—waited at the house for her mother to arrive. Apparently, she would have to go down to the station with them, but they were waiting for someone to accompany her. Carol liked this idea as she didn't much care for driving anyway, and she was pretty sure she was suffering some kind of shock and shouldn't operate a vehicle.

"Are you allowed to display the dead in their home? Or do you have to use a funeral home?" Carol asked the nearest officer when she finally composed herself.

"I don't know, ma'am," he said. He looked to be all of 22 years old.

"Gary wanted his casket to be placed under a large glass top and used as a coffee table at his funeral. He said everyone should use coasters. I suggested we have dry erase markers on hand so we could draw on the glass too. He loved that idea."

"Was your husband expecting to die, ma'am?" asked the detective.

"Yes," Carol said. "Isn't everyone?"

The police said they were unsure of how Gary had died and would need to do an autopsy. They also said she couldn't go to the house yet because it had been ransacked, but she'd might be needed to identify missing objects later.

Carol told them that Gary had nothing worth stealing. She also asked about how the autopsy would impact displaying the body.

"Does he look OK?"

The police looked at each other.

"Gary is deceased, ma'am," the young officer said. The detective nudged him.

"I know that. But does he look good enough to use him as a coffee table? Has his face been marred?"

"We'll go over all that at the station, ma'am."

Carol nodded.

"Did your husband ever mention someone who was out to kill him?" The detective said they would ask questions at the station, but her mother was taking forever. Carol figured the men were bored. They had said foul play was suspected. Gary hadn't planned for that.

"No. No one wanted to kill Gary. Everyone liked him, except my mother, but she's squeamish. She can't even kill flies."

"Why did you and your husband maintain separate residences?" This question came from the younger officer and earned him a glare from the detective.

"They aren't separate," Carol said.

"Why not buy one large house instead of two small houses?" he said, trying again.

"We already had the houses," Carol said.

She was used to telling this story. Carol had inherited this house from her uncle when she was only 18. Gary had purchased his house with lottery winnings when he was 19. They moved into their homes the same day. Gary's parents had been furious that he was just moving out and not giving them any of his money, so they changed the locks and kept all his stuff. He moved in with the contents of his backpack and small car. The rest had been ordered but wouldn't be delivered for a while.

Carol moved into a fully furnished, slightly disheveled house packed with her uncle's things. She invited Gary to sleep in her house until his bed came. After a few celebratory drinks of her uncle's leftover alcohol, she decided Gary should also sleep in her bed. They married the next week at the courthouse. They paid two random people they met at a diner $100 dollars each to be their witnesses and buy them more alcohol.

They were fairly responsible with their inheritance and lottery money. They both went to college and earned degrees. They didn't buy anything extravagant. They mostly lived on the income earned from investments. They got jobs right out of college but lost interest. They didn't need to work and figured it greedy to take jobs other people needed. They travelled some, but neither were the curious or adventurous types. After ten years of marriage, they mostly just hung out at home, dove deeply into strange hobbies, attended AA meetings together, and talked about what they would be when they grew up, which they both knew wouldn't happen. Gary particularly liked to plan his funeral. It was his favorite hobby.

He wanted the refreshments to all be pranks. He loved to make things like cake and frosting that looked like steak and potatoes, and he liked to scoop potatoes so they looked like vanilla ice cream. He also wanted all the drinks served in those cups you can eat. They're a weird, thick, fruit-snack consistency. Gary had ordered them in bulk and used them exclusively for the past year. Carol didn't care for them, but she would have to figure out how to order more. She already had a prank-friendly caterer. Gary found one last week.

"I think he knew he would die young," Carol said. She forgot the police were there. She was actually talking to the narrator in her head. The one that she always pretended was telling hers and Gary's weird little story.

"Was he ill?" the detective asked.

Carol was pretty sure he had already asked this question and scowled at him.

"He knew he would go before me. That's why he told me all his plans. Well, that, and we didn't have a lot of friends. Don't have a lot of friends. He didn't. I don't."

"Are you close with your mother?" the younger officer asked.

"Nope. I'm close to my AA sponsor and my therapist, but those probably don't count."

The police said nothing.

Gary had not anticipated police involvement in his death. He had instructed her to invite his doctors to "the party." Gary started referring to his funeral as "the party" a few years ago. Carol supposed she would be inviting these officers and the coroner instead of doctors.

"Can I get your contact information?" Carol asked. "I will invite you to the party."

The officers exchanged nervous glances and pointed to the business cards they had already set on her coffee table.

"Oh!" she said. "Thank you."

One of the officers excused himself and went to the

kitchen to phone her mother again. Carol knew her mother would take her time. It was early, and that woman never went anywhere unless she was fully made up.

Gary needed a haircut. Carol had bugged him about it yesterday. She was going to have to find out whether a funeral person did that or if she could bring his barber in. Gary was picky about who cut his hair. She needed to make a list so she went to the kitchen to get her notepad and to see what that officer was really up to. The other officer followed her.

"Can I get you a drink?" she asked both of the men, even though one had retreated to the corner while quietly arguing with her mother. "Non alcoholic, of course. I'm an alcoholic. So is Gary. We don't keep that in the houses." She paused. "So *was* Gary."

The officer studied her. She wondered if she'd guessed their ages incorrectly. Carol, herself, looked to be about 25. She was 35, but had a baby face. Gary had a baby face too. They looked like 12-year-olds when they moved into their houses. People were always shocked when she said she'd been married for 17 years.

"I can give you a drink in a cup you can eat," she offered when the officer didn't respond.

"A cup I can eat?"

"Gary. He likes pranks. He thinks these cups are hilarious because he could finish his drink and start eating his glass." She paused again. "He *liked* pranks. He *thought* the cups were hilarious," she corrected. "He played pranks on everyone, even in that article."

"Article?"

Carol frowned. The officer sounded like a parrot. She shrugged it off and began rummaging through papers on the kitchen table and retrieved her notepad.

"I don't think I'll wear a wedding dress. I think I'll wear the pink dress I wore the day we got married. It still fits. It was a little big then."

Carol was telling this to the imaginary narrator too. Gary called the narrator "Bob," but Carol just addressed him directly or referred to him as the narrator. Once again, one of the policemen thought she was addressing them.

"Pardon, ma'am?"

Carol huffed. He was so nosey. "Gary wanted me to wear a wedding dress to the party because I never wore a wedding dress, but that doesn't seem right. I'm not going to do that."

The officer nodded.

Carol was not used to people in her home. She felt like these men were eavesdropping on her life. She looked between the two of them. She hoped they would leave soon.

"Your mother is on her way. She said she'll be here in 15 minutes," said the one officer, hanging up the phone.

"Twenty-five. She thinks she lives 15 minutes away, but she doesn't."

The older officer sighed. Carol wrote "goody bags" on the notepad. Gary wanted elaborate goody bags for guests. He had an online wishlist all set up with quantities. She was pretty sure he had just updated it so all she needed to do was go in and place the order.

"Do you have any more questions for me?" Carol asked. She wanted to do something, but they were making her stand here.

"Yes, ma'am, but we need to discuss those down at the station. We're just waiting for your mother to get here."

"She'll be late."

The younger officer nodded; the older one looked upset.

"I feel as though I should entertain you, but I'd rather not. I'd like to set things in motion for the party. When do you think I will be able to have it?"

"The party?" The older officer clearly hadn't been following along.

"She means the funeral," the younger explained.

"Someone at the station can probably answer that."

"Ok," Carol took several minutes to clear herself a spot at the kitchen table. When she sat, she noticed a bit of newspaper. "This article," she said, retrieving the news clipping.

The younger officer took it to examine it more closely. It was an article about Gary, the eccentric lottery winner turned alcoholic turned sober generous donor to the local clinic.

"This article boasts of Gary's valuables and extensive art collection," the officer said.

"That was the prank! He doesn't have any of that, but they totally bought it." Pause. "*Didn't* have any of that."

The younger officer asked if they could borrow the article. He left the room then returned with it in an evidence bag. They all heard a car door slam.

Carol looked up.

"Why is my mother here?"

Barriers

Many barriers are just for show.
Don't let them stop you.

Artist: Rebecca Eve Schweitzer

Rosary

Rebecca Eve Schweitzer

I threw away a rosary
yesterday caked in dust
and dead bugs addressed
to a woman who is no longer
here

I wondered later what other
treasure hid among the lost
mangled and forgotten
in the abyss between wall
and desk

I didn't think about the prayers
thrown away with broken binders
and a cracked calculator
I only considered the rush
to clean

I wondered later if anyone
would want to grasp those beads
after they sat in grime and fly
carcasses or if that life gave them
more potency

I barely noticed the package
guilting the careless addressee
into praying and paying
for the orphaned sick hungry
lost or something

I wondered later if rosaries
packaged for guilt and money
would taint the prayers asked for
or did the prayer maker's heart
matter more

I wonder now if prayers
packaged in routine fail
to reach their destination
or if the act itself is
enough

Weam Namou

Weam Namou is an Eric Hoffer award-winning author of 13 books, an award-winning filmmaker, journalist, poet, and lecturer. She's a TV host and an Ambassador for the Authors Guild of America [Detroit Chapter], the oldest and largest writing organization in the United States.

Namou is a graduate of best-selling author Lynn Andrews' four-year course of study and training in the sacred healing arts. She's the founder of the Path of Consciousness, a spiritual and writing retreat, and Unique Voices in Films, a 501(C)(3) nonprofit organization. www.weamnamou.com

A Levantine Drink

Weam Namou

At night, we smelled my father's *arak* all the way
from the other side of the room.

My younger brother and I
sprawled on the rugs, watching television,
as he lounged on the couch in his *dishdasha*
and drank that unsweetened, anise-flavored beverage.

After a hard day's work,
he ate his supper with a glass of liquor,
and fell asleep on the couch in front of the news
which by then had become long bars of noisy color.

These memories of Baghdad still buzz around me like a bee,
despite me having detached from Iraq's soil decades ago,
and more recently, from its political and religious ideology.

I can detach, I suppose, but never be indifferent
to the smell of *arak*, for instance, or the Levantine cuisine
that I and the women in my tribe still cook
in our American kitchens,
the stuffed baby eggplants and cookies filled
with dates or walnuts, and sometimes sprinkled with sugar.

Little Baghdad

Weam Namou

As I opened the door to enter the produce market,
the whiff of the Iraqi flat bread, made in a Tanoor oven,
carried me off to my childhood days in Baghdad.
The baker hadn't yet started the fire this morning,
but the day-in and day-out of the ingredients
that formed the diamond-shaped bread
caused flour dust and baking powder in the air.

Once inside, the door now closed,
Baghdad's memories captured my senses,
separating me from my home in the suburbs of
Metro Detroit.

The place was silent.

The Arabic music they normally played hadn't yet begun.

I packed the shopping cart with tomatoes,

English cucumbers,

jalapeno peppers, clotted cream, and chocolate croissants,

remembering my mother whose once Christian village in

northern Iraq was recently destroyed by invaders.

That land's history keeps repeating itself.

I set the items on the counter. The cashier greeted me,

as she does all her female customers,

in endearing Arabic or Aramaic terms of *love* or *dear*.

We chitchatted briefly before I walked out into the

Metro Detroit city I've lived in for decades,

Sterling Heights—

now nicknamed "Little Baghdad."

Teresa Moy

Teresa Moy is a technical writer, tai chi and qigong instructor, and lover of learning. She graduated from California State University, Sacramento, with a degree in English.

Since 2006, Moy has lived in Oakland County where she telecommutes from her home office and teaches classes in Rochester Hills and Oxford Township. She enjoys traveling and photography to experience life from different perspectives.

Writing Scared

Teresa Moy

Adrien leaned out the open window of his second-story apartment, scanning street activities for writing ideas. A customer banged on the door of the grocery store, desperate for a last-minute item, but the grocer shook his head and pointed to the closed sign. In the nearby park, a woman jogged up the gazebo stairs as a groundskeeper popped up from behind the trash cans, removing garbage bags. Two boys played with broken branches they found by the pond.

The writer closed his eyes. He envisioned the shopper pounding on the door, begging the grocer to save her from a crazy madman. He pictured the groundskeeper slinking after the jogger. He imagined the boys engaging in a life-and-death battle, their steel swords clashing together.

Adrien put on his reading glasses and flipped through the papers strewn across his desk, searching for chapters that might work best with his victim, stalker, and warriors. As he wrote, he unleashed his paranoid mind. Every soft sound, tiny creak, and dark corner meant danger or a signal to run.

"None of you are safe," he whispered to his characters.

As the evening began, the apartment contracted and settled against the cool air like a giant, slow exhale. Adrien twitched at the natural groans and creaks. Even the plumbing chimed in, with periodic rattles and whistles. He kept glimpsing out of his study where he swore an unknown presence had passed. He grabbed his whiskey glass and shook out the last clinging drops.

Tossing and turning that night in bed, Adrien spent the first hour quieting his protagonist, villain, and love interest. They offered scenarios where they prevailed or died. They dragged him to the park where the cheery foliage became a secluded forest and the pond transformed into a murky lake.

He screwed his eyes shut. "Please, stop."

After he smacked his characters into submission, the spooky twilight cracking and popping agitated his mind. The nefarious, unknown presence haunted him out of the corner of his eye, from inside his closets, or behind his headboard. With sheer exhaustion, he confronted a faceless, black-cloaked figure who clawed at him. To escape, Adrien charged over a cliff to jolt himself awake.

So the night persisted, like every night.

The next afternoon, he left his apartment and headed downstairs. The dim staircase squeaked and sagged under his footsteps. There were no handrails. Adrien worried one day the unknown presence might just push him down the stairs.

He ordered a black coffee from the first-floor bakery and told the barista to add two espresso shots. He drank his liquid caffeine and shuffled to the grocery store. The grocer eyed the four whiskey bottles Adrien brought to the counter.

Cranky from sleep deprivation, he scowled and thrust down crumpled bills. "What are you looking at?"

He stepped out of the store and noticed heavy, ominous gray clouds looming overhead. The first raindrops bounced off his head and shoulders. People opened umbrellas, covered up with jackets, and ducked into stores. But one person, a willowy young woman with chocolate brown hair, lifted her face to the sky. She stretched out her arms to embrace the drops as they kissed her cheeks. Adrien stood under a building overhang and watched her. No harm, he thought, would dare challenge this angelic figure.

When the light sprinkle changed into a downpour, he returned to his apartment. The clattering rain, lightning flashes, and rumbling thunder put him in a gloomy mood, perfect for dark writing. Adrien took a swig of his whiskey. Recalling the jogger, the groundskeeper, and the shopper from yesterday, he wrote:

"As Charlotte rushed up the stairs to her mother's room, a disheveled, hunched man stepped out from behind the tall bookcase and crept after her. 'Mama!' she cried, jiggling the locked doorknob."

Steps echoed in his head, and the writer paused. The apartment was silent except for the clock ticking. He scribbled:

"The creaking floorboards made her turn, and she jumped at the sight of the leering man. Dull, sunken eyes seared through her. His grin revealed yellow-stained, crooked teeth. She pressed her body against the door, her fists pounding."

Adrien flinched and dropped his pen, which fell to the floor and rolled several feet away. Was the banging in his mind or his apartment? The knock rapped again, and he realized someone was at his front door.

"May I help you?" Looking through the peephole, he faltered. The woman he'd seen earlier, her upturned face welcoming the rain, peered at him.

"I'm Leora. Your new housekeeper and cook?"

The storm had dwindled, and the sunshine created a halo around her dark, sopping hair and fair complexion. She was a twenty something with a plain countenance, but her soft eyes and bright smile warmed him and lightened his mood.

"Yes, of course. I forgot you were coming today." He unfastened the locks, lifted the latch, and unhooked the chain. He opened the door and waved her inside.

Adrien showed Leora around the apartment, and she nodded in response to his monologue. Her silence pleased him; he disliked inane chatter that polluted the air. The tour ended in his study with a brusque admonition to leave his desk alone.

The niceties covered, she offered to get groceries and return to make dinner. Adrien gave her a couple twenties and a copy of the apartment key.

"Don't disturb me until supper is ready."

"No worries. I'm here to help you."

The wordsmith retreated to his study and read his last sentence. Charlotte and the crazed, dentist-deprived madman awaited their next move. The scene would end with the man killing her, and her demise would be gruesome with plentiful screaming. Or should he give her super adrenaline strength or weapons disguised as everyday household items? Which outcome did his readers expect?

Whiskey glass in hand, he worked on a draft of both scenarios. He didn't know how much time had passed when shuffling footsteps and thumping filtered into his head.

"Leora?"

He walked to the kitchen, but no one was there. Were his written pages talking to him? Fresh in the author's mind, Charlotte was thrashing the madman with a steel mop, using a move she learned in her self-defense class. Adrien grabbed a broom and listened to the stillness, determined to grapple with the unknown presence who violated his sanity.

The front door opened. He yelped and raised the broom. Leora jumped. She clutched the grocery bags in her hands.

Adrien cleared his throat, straightened his jacket, and lowered the broom. "Here, let me help you." He sensed the unknown presence shrinking into the walls.

Leora arranged cooking oils and spices on a shelf that was bare save the whiskey bottles Adrien had bought that afternoon. He was embarrassed, but she didn't seem to care. When she also set out a small orchid and sandalwood incense sticks, he frowned.

"To clear and lighten the air," she explained. "It's rather

heavy in here."

After dinner, Adrien sipped his whiskey as he watched Leora bustle about the kitchen. His eyes droopy, he lumbered to the living room and plopped on the sofa.

Sinking heavier into slumber, he saw his nightmare nemesis emerge. The black-cloaked creature wrapped its gnarled fingers around his neck. Adrien grasped at its hands and struggled to pull them from his throat. He peered down the vast, dark hole that was its face. An eerie screech emitted from deep within its bowels.

"No, go away! Leave me alone!"

From a distance, a small, nebulous gold light appeared. It drew nearer and mesmerized him as it changed colors— yellow, green, blue, purple, and silver. It pulsated like a beating heart, filling Adrien with a pleasant warmth and calming the angst in his chest.

Putting all his energy and resolve into this soft glow, he looked back at his nemesis. It was the same figure draped in a black cloak, but it had lost its malevolence. Adrien released his hold and expanded his arms. The creature loosened its grip. Left with no one to torture, it disintegrated into tiny dust particles that reformed into white doves and flew away.

Adrien's eyes popped open. How had he escaped without the usual drastic measures of mangling, crushing, or killing himself to end his nightmares? Every other night, he'd awaken with a jolt, wipe the sweat off his face, slug some whiskey, and rock himself back to sleep.

A sweet murmur glided along the still night air, and Adrien followed its trail. It led him to the balcony where the French doors stood ajar, and he saw Leora leaning against the iron railing, singing to herself. She turned at the sound of his footsteps and smiled.

Then, the author understood. Fighting his fears or numbing them with alcohol had never been the answer. He had to surrender. But how much of this magical solution was her doing? How much was his?

He stared into her brown, peaceful eyes. "You must never leave."

Fresh Eyes

Teresa Moy

My eyes flit to the brain loft, flames licking out of the windows. Charred remnants of my scribbled notes fall lifeless from the sky while firefighters aim their fire hoses to squelch the blaze. My neighbors gather on the street, pointing, gawking, and covering their mouths.

I park my car and jump out. As I dash to my house, blackened paper memories brush against my face, taunting me. What caused this destruction? Was it my doing? WHERE IS LING?

"Oh, Jessie," says a neighbor. "This is just awful."

"We're so sorry," offers another couple as if someone has died. "Please call us if there's anything we can do. We're only two houses away."

I stare at them but say nothing. I tunnel through my mind, digging through folders of mental images, but conjure up a disappointing blank. They are strangers.

~ ~ ~

Earlier that morning, I pieced together my life. I woke up with Ling curled up at the foot of my bed, swishing her fluffy tail and meowing. A silk brocade journal, decorated with red and gold dragonflies stitched into the fabric, sat on my nightstand. "*Read me,*" said a note attached to the journal. The note was in my handwriting, but I didn't remember writing it.

I headed to the kitchen to prepare my morning tea, and similar messages greeted me on the walls, windows, and dinette table. I added jasmine leaves and steaming water to my gaiwan cup. As I sipped my tea, I opened the journal.

"Today is Friday, October 12, 1990. You have ten appointments this afternoon at Hair Cutters Salon. No other commitments. If you're confused, you still experience intermittent amnesia triggered by a small two-engine plane crash on October 12, 1985. Searchers found you by the side of the highway near Hiawatha National Forest, but they never recovered the plane or your parents."

I knew this house and the salon, so my memory was intact. But my upper lip quivered at the thought of my parents. I looked at their empty places at the table, and my tears splashed into my tea and created little ripples. I imagined my father winking at me over the newspaper in his hands, and my mother singing as she put a comforting arm around me. I missed the smell of her stir-fried baby bok choy, eggplant with garlic sauce, and dumplings. Wait, how did I lose five years?

"Everything you need is in the loft. Have a wonderful day. Love yourself. Be amazing."

These parting words accompanied my parents' big hugs whenever I went off to college, started a new job, or began any adventure. *Love yourself*, my mother would say. *Be amazing*, my father would say right after her.

Flipping back a few pages, I recognized my routine – the daily bike rides, the biweekly grocery shopping, and the weekly housecleaning. But my conversations with neighbors, the grocer, and clients were a revelation.

I ascended the stairs up to the loft, which was my mother's art studio. My favorite painting, a lotus on a koi pond, still adorned the wall facing the street. But nothing else looked the same. Instead of easels, canvases, and paint palettes, I saw plain shelves lining one wall from floor to ceiling, weighed down by rows of manila folders. Maps, notes, and photos tacked to a large cork board covered the opposite wall. I noticed the Chinese characters for "dragonfly," drawn on rice paper with my mother's gentle brush strokes, next to names of people I didn't know.

What did all this mess mean? What kind of project was I working on?

"I guess this place is my brain loft," I said to Ling, who responded with a lazy yawn. She was the only familiar, comforting presence in my life.

The folders were organized in labeled sections. "Household," "Hair Cutters Salon," "Daily Activities." I pulled the ones for my clients and sat at the desk, pushing aside the lucky bamboo plant and mandarin spice candle to make room.

I studied my memories like I was cramming for an exam. But the more I fed the words into my brain, the more confused I became. The names blurred with hair styles, occupations, hobbies, and goals. The volume of detail crowded my mind and pressed against my ears, threatening to gush out. My head hurt. I cried aloud and banged my fists on the table, and Ling darted out of the brain loft. I feared I wouldn't be able to keep my notes straight, and everyone would discover my secret.

To my great relief, an easy solution materialized. I could do what any desperate student would do—write the answers on my arms and check them before each appointment. As I rolled up my sleeves, I found cheat notes from yesterday. I scrubbed my upper arms until they became a reddish clean slate and scribbled a fresh layer of verbiage.

I am in control, I told myself as I left the comfort and safety of my home. *Love yourself, be amazing*, I added, wiping a tear off my cheek.

~ ~ ~

An ash flutters past my face, reeling me back to the present. So much of my memories and my life, preserved on

71

shelves of manila folders, gone. I clutch my hair as my eyes search for Ling.

A firefighter approaches me to state the obvious. "Ma'am, the fire started in the loft, and it was badly damaged. But I believe the rest of the house is salvageable. Any idea how it started?"

Earlier in the evening, I had lit the candle in the brain loft to replace the scent of salon products in my nostrils. I caress my bandaged finger, the one responsible for making me abandon both my house and cat.

"I was chopping vegetables for dinner," I mumble. "I cut my finger and had to drive to urgent care. The candle upstairs—I forgot about it."

I want to tell the firefighter I'm a conscientious person. I check the stove, windows, and doors three times before leaving the house. Sometimes I return to make sure the garage door is closed. But if I lose Ling, I can never forgive myself.

"Do you have somewhere to stay?" he asks. "At least for a couple days?"

"This is so terrible," says a neighbor, coming over to hug me, and I flinch. If I even had a manila folder for her, it's now destroyed. I touch my arm, but I have no secret notes to help me. "If you like, you can stay with us tonight." When I hesitate, the woman adds, "Please. We insist."

I shift my attention to a tall, slender man who is approaching. I know him; his name is Conner. He's with a young girl whom I don't recognize, but she has my traumatized cat. I cry with joy, and Ling wriggles out of the girl's arms as I take her in mine. This woman must be Conner's new wife, and the girl his stepdaughter.

"She'll stay with us for now," he assures the firefighter. They continue their conversation, but it's a jumbled mess of words to my ears. I hold Ling against my chest, and her warmth soothes my frazzled mind. *Thank you, God,* I keep saying under my breath.

Conner interrupts my thoughts when the firefighter leaves. "Please, Jessie. We have a spare room. It's no trouble."

He gestures toward his house, but when I don't move, he leads me by the elbow, followed by his wife and daughter. We walk to a white two-story with a wooden hanging bench swing and bamboo wind chimes. I see "421" next to the front door. I remember this porch but can't pinpoint why.

"Ophelia, why don't you show Jessie to the guest room?"

The girl leads me upstairs and down the hallway. I sit on the bed, and the fluffy down comforter billows around me. The rug is so luxurious I can curl my toes up in it. I smell lavender. These surroundings also seem familiar which makes me uneasy.

Ophelia whispers, "How come?"

"How come what?" I whisper back.

"How come you stopped Operation Dragonfly?" She looks hopeful.

This question baffles me. I don't know what Operation Dragonfly is, but I recall the journal and the mysterious cork board, both with images of dragonflies. I had intended to study the board this evening, but it was now burnt to a crisp. "Quite honestly, I have no idea."

"Don't you want to find your parents?"

The back of my neck prickles. I open my mouth to speak, but no words form. After a few moments, I say, "What do you know about my mom and dad?"

She furrows her brow and purses her lips. She leans in toward me. "Conner stole the flight plans. He's hiding them in the basement. The plane, your parents—they didn't just disappear. The search team was looking in the wrong place."

L. Broas Mann

L. Broas Mann received mechanical engineering degrees from Illinois Institute of Technology and Northwestern University. That was followed by a fifty-year career at Chrysler Corporation engaged in automotive engine research, during which time he wrote many technical papers and reports.

Upon retiring, Mann wanted to continue working with words and ideas, so he turned to writing historical fiction and published three books about the history of his family's pioneering adventures in western Michigan. Early on, he also dabbled in poetry, not the classic form but the kind that tells a story.

Rehearsal

L. Broas Mann

In they stumbled, raucous, loud -
teens in jeans, old sweatshirts.
  Jabbering, joking, laughing;
  sprawled on wooden tiers.

Sister was punctual, neat, precise -
her entrance signaled work would begin.
  sopranos in back
        basses between
    altos up front, tenors off right.

Sixty-six ears locked onto her pipe
as she pitched the note that tuned them in.
  She raised a hand; they transformed
  into one mind under her command.

Arms sweeping in broad arcs,
she drew out voices like threads to a loom;
  weaving melody into lyric,
  creating patterns of deep harmony.

The hymn drifted off on a soft high note,
floating away like a wisp of smoke.
  She sighed, "That's the best you've ever done;
  I'm sure even Seraphim loved the sound."

The Chaperone

L. Broas Mann

it wasn't junk food
or lukewarm pop;
it wasn't the smell
of sweat, beer and pot.

and it wasn't the music
all raucous and loud
that made her cringe from
the unwashed crowd.

the thing she abhorred
in this howling horde
was the pubescent screech
of each vocal cord.

the assault on her ears
would somehow inure,
but the noise in her brain
she could not endure.

the shrieks and screams
she had to erase;
so in panic and guilt
she fled from the place.

her car was an oven
all closed up tight,
but it offered refuge
at the end of her flight.

plunged into silence,
she drank in the peace
and prayed that the noise
in her head would now cease.

she remembered Woodstock:
"it was never like this"
but then, forty years

       is quite an abyss.

Mel Werner

Mel Werner is retired from engineering and now enjoys pursuing his hobbies which include painting, organic gardening, weight lifting, and writing.

After having several poems and short stories published, he is close to finishing his first book, titled *Twin*.

The "Kingdom of Googol" is his first children's story.

Kingdom of Googol

Mel Werner

There was a knock on the door. The thirty-six-year-old woman put her laptop down, went to the door and opened it.

"Daddy, what y'all doin here this late at night? Come on in out of the rain."

Her father folded his umbrella and leaned it by the door. "Late at night? It's only nine o'clock. I wanted to visit my granddaughter before she goes to bed."

"You're going to be here Saturday for her eighth birthday party, aren't you?"

"I'll be here, but I wanted some one-on-one time with her before the party."

"I was just on the computer googling birthday party games. It's Neves's bedtime, but I can hear her playing up there. Go on up. Maybe you can get her to go to sleep."

"Googling?"

"It's a way of searching for something on the computer."

He made his way upstairs and peeked into her bedroom. "Neves, honey, wha'cha doin?"

"Grandpa! I'm playing with my alphabet blocks. See what I made?"

On top of her dresser five blocks spelled her name, Neves.

He stared at the blocks for a moment, then said, "It's nine fifteen. You should be sleeping."

"I don't want to go to bed, Grandpa. Tomorrow in school we're having an arithmetic test. I hate arithmetic. If I don't go to bed, tomorrow won't come."

"No, honey, it doesn't work that way. How about you hop into bed, and Grandpa tells you a story?"

"A story? Okay, what's the story about?"

He looked at the rain hitting her window then he turned to the blocks again. He tucked her in, and then started. "It's about a birthday party in the Kingdom of Googol."

"Googol. That's a funny name."

"It may sound funny, but Googol was a serious place with a serious problem."

"What kind of problem?"

"Well, a googol is a number with a hundred zeros behind it, and numbers were very important to the Kingdom of Googol. You need numbers to live."

"How do you mean, Grandpa?"

"I'll tell you."

~ ~ ~

Hundreds of years ago when Princess Fifen came of age on her eighteenth birthday, there were celebrations. The streets were filled with festivals. The palace was covered in decorations. Her brothers gave her gifts. That evening, there would be a birthday ball. Now, the future queen was considered an adult; she would have responsibilities.

On the morning of her birthday, the captain of the palace guard took Fifen on a tour of the kingdom. He showed her things she had never known, and he filled her in on her new responsibilities.

They came to a courtyard where a dozen young men were sword fighting. She asked the captain about the fighting. "What are those men doing?"

"Those young men are training to be your father's royal guards."

As they walked closer a young man stopped fighting, smiled at the princess, and bowed.

"Captain, do you know who that boy is?"

"Yes, my lady, I've helped train them all. That boy has promise. He's smart and he trains hard. He comes from a poor family of farmers. I have great hopes that someday he could become a guardsman."

"Can I talk to him, Captain? Would he talk to me?"

"Would he talk to you? I'm sure he would be honored, Princess. He will have something to tell his future grandchildren."

They walked up to the group. As they approached, the practicing stopped and they all bowed down on one knee.

The captain spoke, "Rise, Soldier Octen. The princess wishes to address you."

"Good day, Soldier, my name is Princess Fifen." She put out her hand.

Octen grabbed her hand and shook it up and down vigorously like he would a man's.

The Captain shook his head. "Mister Octen, the proper way to greet a future queen is to kiss her ring hand, not pump her hand like you are drawing water from a well. I apologize for him, Princess."

"That's quite alright, Captain. I'm sure this soldier's training does not include palace etiquette."

"I beg your pardon, Princess Fifen." The young soldier's eyes lit up. "Is not Fifen the ancient way to say the number five?"

"You are observant; I received my name because throughout history I am only the fifth female born to the royal family."

The handsome boy responded, "There's plenty of girls in our family, but none as fair as you, Fifen." He bowed again.

The captain interrupted, "That's Princess Fifen. The lady has a title, Soldier!"

"That's all right, Captain," said the blushing princess. "I find his talk refreshing, even if it's not proper. Soldier Octen, I would like you to attend my birthday ball in the palace tonight."

"I would be honored; Princess Fifen, but I do not have the proper attire."

"Princess, this man is a serf, from a family of peasants; he would not fit with the royal family."

"Captain, I am of age. Am I not allowed to make decisions? Do I not have the right to pick my own guests?"

"Of course, you do, Princess. It is my turn to apologize. I will personally see to it this man is dressed for the occasion."

"Thank you. I will see the both of you at my party tonight."

With that statement, Princess Fifen and the captain continued their tour.

That evening the ball began. Hundreds of lanterns lit the great hall. The royal orchestra of forty musicians played as guests arrived by carriage. As they walked in, they were announced then greeted by King Maximillion and Queen Trillion.

Soldier Octen and the captain arrived together; they were greeted by a lesser group of dignitaries, counts and noblemen.

Octen was dressed similar to the captain. He wore a red jacket with eight brass buttons. Gold braids were looped and fastened under his shoulder epaulets. His black pants had a single red stripe down each side. A dueling saber hung on his hip and he held a tricorn hat in his hand. The handsome young soldier turned all the female heads in the hall.

When all the guests were greeted, the music stopped. Then the orchestra began to play the Kingdom's anthem. Three chairs sat on a raised platform. An empty chair was positioned between the seated king and queen. Maximillion stood and walked off the platform and took the hand of his daughter. He led her back onto the platform.

"People of Googol, may I proudly introduce to you, our future queen, Princess Fifen."

The audience of hundreds roared with delight.

Princess Fifen wore a pale blue silk dress. Its collar, cuffs, and hem were covered with thousands of tiny white gemstones. It sparkled like it was dipped in stardust.

Octen was mesmerized by her beauty. He could not wait to talk to her. Unfortunately, he did wait. It was impossible to get within twenty feet of the birthday princess. She was constantly surrounded by dozens of counts, princes, and noble men. They brought her petit fours and drinks; they talked, laughed, and danced with her.

As the night went on, never did Princess Fifen so much as look at the young soldier.

Why did she invite me? Am I nothing when compared to the elite of Googol? I should not have come.

Halfway through the ball the orchestra played a waltz. King Maximillion danced with his daughter. The floor cleared and the crowd was quiet as they circled. Before the waltz ended the king returned to his throne. Princess Fifen walked down a line of handsome suitors, picking her next dance partner. One by one she passed by them all, and walked to the far side of the hall where she reached out her hand to Octen.

This time, he kissed her hand and they danced. All through the night, they never parted. Clearly, they enjoyed each other's company.

Late in the night, the king spoke to the captain. "Who is that young soldier, Number One? Why is he here?"

"Your daughter invited him when she met him on her morning tour. She insisted even when I objected, your Excellency."

"Yes, Fifen is headstrong. Let them have their fun, but after tonight see to it their paths never cross again."

"Yes, your Majesty, you have my word." The captain knew even a palace guard would have to do something heroic to even be allowed to talk to a princess, and Octen was only a guard in training.

Anyway, the princess and soldier talked and danced all night. Some said they even kissed when the ball ended. When they parted, Octen went to his barracks where his division lived. Both were so excited they could not sleep that night. Because the ball ended late, both were allowed to sleep into the next day. It was a good day to sleep, because it rained all day. This was not just an ordinary rain; it rained hard for three days and two nights.

The people of Googol were hardy folk. They had work to do, so the rain did not stop them. They went about their day going to school, farming and selling at the marketplace, even though they got wet.

~ ~ ~

"They got wet from the rain, Grandpa?"

"Yes, it was a long time ago, before the invention of the umbrella. There was something very different about this rain. The rain burned their skin. Not like fire, but it was irritating; it made them itch."

~ ~ ~

One of Maximillon's royal guards was the first to show the rain's harmful effects. When the downpour caused the Kingdom's river to flood, the brave man jumped in and swam to the other side to open the flood gates. From being immersed in rain water, he began to itch even more than the others.

~ ~ ~

"What's immersed, Grandpa?"

"Immersed means he was covered in water, sweetie."

~ ~ ~

Anyway, the next day he broke out in a red, itchy rash. As the days passed, the rash formed numbers on his skin. On his arm was a number four, his chest a number nine, and on his forehead the number three appeared.

Time passed and more people had the same condition. The numbers varied and so did their locations, but all the people had the same miserable itching. Eventually, all Googol's people were afflicted, even the royal family. They called for the Kingdom's best physicians. They tried herbal teas and they tried poultices made of mud, roots, and powders. Nothing worked. The problem only got worse.

When the guardsman who was first inflicted was summoned to appear before the king's best doctors at twelve noon, he never showed up. King Maximillion was furious; he sent his palace guard to get him. They found him totally confused, sitting in his room staring at his clock. He could no longer tell time. He could read numbers, but to him they had no meaning.

Weeks passed and the new problem spread until the whole Kingdom of tens of thousands could not understand numbers.

~ ~ ~

"Grandpa, why was it so bad? Who cares about numbers?"
"Oh, it was very bad."

~ ~ ~

Not only could no one tell time, no one could count, add or subtract. When the townspeople went to the marketplace, the storekeepers did not know how much to charge. They could not sell their goods, so people stole what they needed. Workers could not be paid, so they stopped working. Taxes could not be collected, so the Kingdom was falling apart.

Something had to be done; people were starving for lack of food. They were afraid to drink the water, so they became dehydrated. They were on the verge of dying.

The good King Maximillion gathered the wisest subjects in the land of Googol. There were physicians, storytellers, and professors. Together they had no answers, but one old woman told a story of Googol hundreds of years earlier. Daughters were very rare in the royal family. Fifen was only the fifth one known in the family's history. Hundreds of years before when the fourth girl was born, that king was so happy he announced the princess would be queen. The trouble was she had an older brother. As the first born, he felt it was his right to be the next king. For generations, this was the tradition. The son felt the king had no right to deny him.

His father reminded him as king he had every right to change the law.

The first born son could not accept his father's ruling. He made trouble, inciting riots. He even tried to overthrow his own father.

The king had no choice but to banish his son from the Kingdom of Googol.

The first born son moved to Mount Prime. There he would practice wizardry for the rest of his days. Because he was no longer considered the first in line, he was known as Wizard Zero. From the mountain top, Zero would cast evil spells on the Kingdom of Googol.

Fortunately, the Kingdom had wizards of its own and each spell was broken by the good wizards.

Dozens of years passed and Zero's powers multiplied. During his sister's rule as queen, Zero cast a spell that could not be broken. He stood on his mountain during a thunderstorm and cast his most powerful curse. He shouted, "If numbers are not important, then numbers will no longer exist."

The rain came down on Googol and the curse started to take effect on the land. Once again the queen summoned the kingdom's wizards, but wizardry was becoming obsolete. All powerful wizards were gone. The best the remaining wizards could do was to delay the curse until the next princess came of age. That time was now, during the time of Princess Fifen, two hundred years later.

It was rumored every evil spell had a good spell that could break it. King Maximillion listened to the old woman. Her advice was to go to the top of Mount Prime and find Wizard Zero's book of spells and destroy it. He called for his Captain of the Guard. "Number One, gather together all of our able bodied soldiers. We are going on a mission to Mount Prime. We're going to end this curse on Googol."

"Your Majesty, most of our army is disabled from the curse. How many soldiers do you need?"

Maximillion looked confused. "How many? How many? Do not ask me for a number. Bring all you can find!"

The captain returned the next day with only three others with him. "I apologize, my King, only these few are able to make the journey."

The king stood up and unsheathed his sword. "Only these few? I will go with you."

Maximillion's twin sons walked forward. "No, Father, you stay with our people. We will go in your stead."

With that statement, one of the twins passed out from dehydration.

Princess Fifen stood from her chair. "I will take my brother's place."

"My daughter, you are our Kingdom's future. I forbid it."

"My Father, if the curse is not broken, Googol has no future."

"Even with you Fifen, the numbers seem small. It is rumored the mountain is protected by griffins."

The captain spoke, "My King, there is another, but you may not want him." The captain signaled and Octen walked into the great hall.

They had been forbidden to see each other since the ball. Fifen threw her arms around him. "Octen, it's so wonderful to see you! Yes, Father, together we will break this curse."

The next morning, stocked with the best food, drink, and weapons the kingdom could supply, the seven brave warriors started their quest to Mount Prime. They hiked all day, and at night they made camp at the foot of Mount Prime. For dinner, they had potatoes and dried beef. It was a good meal; they needed it for tomorrow's climb to the top of Prime.

They dare not drink water, so they had packed bottles of wine. Fifen and Octen went to sleep holding hands. When Fifen heard a noise, she opened her eyes. Two black shadows passed over them.

"Octen, Octen, wake up!"

"I'm awake, Princess. What's wrong?"

"I saw two big birds fly over us. Did you see them?"

"I did not; we drank a lot of wine. Maybe you are feeling its effects?"

"Maybe a little, but I saw something. Do griffins fly?"

"I do not know. Get some sleep. I will watch the sky."

The next morning they had a quick breakfast then started their climb up the mountain. At half past noon, they stopped at a plateau near the top of Prime.

While they rested, the captain sharpened his sword.

One of the other soldiers approached him. "Why bother sharpening your sword, Captain? I have the sharpest blade in the Kingdom. Watch this." The boastful Guardsman, Alanine, drew his sword. He stood next to a tree and with a mighty blow his sword cut the five inch thick tree down.

"Alanine, you do not show me the sharpness of your blade. You show me the strength of your arm. Watch and learn. Princess Fifen, may I borrow a silk scarf?"

The captain of the guard lifted the scarf high and dropped it. As it gently floated down he held his blade under it. The silk passed over the blade and was cut in half. The group of six were amazed.

There was a shriek in the sky, and then from behind, three inch talons sunk into each of the captain's shoulders. The griffin lifted him off the ground and started to fly away.

~ ~ ~

"Grandpa, what's a griffin?"

"A griffin is a legendary creature with the body of a lion and the head, wings, and talons of an eagle."

~ ~ ~

The captain swung his sharp sword from side to side. Feathers flew and the tips of the griffin's wings were cut off. They crashed to the ground with the eight hundred pound griffin on top.

The entire group charged the beast, striking it repeatedly. The blows seemed to have no effect, and just as the griffin's powerful beak went for the captain's neck, Alanine's mighty arms swung his sword, cutting off the beast's head.

There was no time to rest; the second griffin ran down the mountain path. It threw the princess's brother off the path and came shrieking at Fifen. Octen threw himself between them; his sword chopped and stabbed at the monster, one, two, three, four times. The griffin's right talons ripped at Octen, putting deep scratches in his iron shield. With its other talons, it struck Octen's right hand ripping the sword from it. The twenty-one year old soldier fell on his back with no weapon to defend himself.

Like a lion, the beast sprang into the air pouncing toward Octen.

Princess Fifen screamed, "Octen, use this." She threw him a spear.

Catching it he pointed the spear upward, bracing its end to the ground. The weight of the eight hundred pound beast drove the six foot weapon completely through it. The second griffin fell dead next to a wounded Octen.

After resting and regrouping, the seven continued to the top of the mountain. Finally, the seven battered warriors climbed a stairway of thirteen steps that took them onto a covered platform. Its hexagon shape had six stone pillars, one at each corner. In the center of the platform, the Wizard Zero's book of spells floated four feet off the ground. The leather bound book was open and red numbers streamed out of it. They passed between two of the pillars and flew toward the land of Googol.

The captain was the first to approach the book, but before

he got close he collapsed from his wounds. Fifen went to him and cradled his head in her lap.

Octen was the next to try. He limped toward the open book. He felt he did not have the energy to walk around to read it, so he reached out and rotated it one hundred and eighty degrees. The evil book burnt his fingers and he quickly released it. Octen started to read Wizard Zero's writing. The words written in blood described the curse. There was no doubt this was exactly what Googol suffered.

The words on the opposite page were in a different color. They were directions to stop the curse. He read them out loud. "To save the land of Googol, the task is very simple. Count your fingers on your right hand and with that hand close the book." Octen looked at his hand, confusion showed on his face. He could not count.

One by one the others did the same; none were able to follow the book's directions.

Without counting his fingers, Octen tried to close the book. The book, again, burnt his hand, much more than before. He pulled his hand back and examined his burns. To his surprise a small number appeared on the back of his smallest finger. It had no meaning but he read it anyway. "One," he said out loud.

The floating book wavered up and down. Again he felt a burning on his second finger. The number appeared. "Two," said Octen. The words in the book became bright red and the numbers stopped streaming from it. He felt encouraged; on his middle finger he read a number. "Three," he shouted. The book began to smolder. Octen looked at the next finger, nothing, then slowly it appeared. "Four," he again shouted.

The group looked excited as smoke poured from the evil book.

Octen's thumb also burned with pain but it was bloodied from the griffin's attack. He wiped it clean on his shirt. The skin was gone and even though it burned like the others, no number appeared. Octen desperately searched his wounded thumb. When he found nothing on his thumb, he turned to the group. "I'm sorry, there's no number." Then he looked at the princess, knowing their future was dead. "I'm sorry, Fifen."

Speaking Fifen, the ancient word for five, the book burst into flames. Octen grabbed it with his right hand. Even though the book was consumed in fire, it felt cool. He slammed it shut.

In seconds, a pile of ashes fell to the ground. The numbers on their faces and bodies instantly disappeared. The itching and confusion stopped. The curse was broken.

When they returned to the palace, Octen was made a Royal Palace Guard. Within a year he married the future Queen Fifen. It has been said Queen Fifen and Prince Octen had a dozen children, all boys.

~ ~ ~

"And they lived happily ever after," said a smiling Neves. "You know, Grandpa, our town has a river and there's a big mountain only a few miles away."

"The Kingdom of Googol is now Goodone, Tennessee? Anything's possible. Time to go to sleep now, honey." He turned off the bedside lamp and kissed her on the forehead. "And don't worry about that test tomorrow."

"I'll do well, Grandpa. Arithmetic's important." In the dark she saw him walk to her dresser. He stood there for a moment and then Neves heard faint sliding sounds. He then walked out of her room and into the hallway.

"That was a good story, even if it's not real. Leave the hallway light on, Grandpa Max."

"I will, Princess. Goodnight."

As Neves lay in bed, her eyes slowly became adjusted to the dim light. She looked at the top of her dresser. He had rearranged the five alphabet blocks that spelled her name.

They were in reverse order and now read SEVEN.

Danielle Bernock

Danielle Bernock is an international, award-winning author. Her works include *Emerging With Wings*, "A Bird Named Payn," and "Love's Manifesto." She is dedicated to sharing her words that encourage and transform people's lives.

When she's not writing, she loves to spend time with her family and friends, be walking or playing out in nature, or reading a good book. Bernock is a member of the Tribe Writers and Rochester Writers.

Publication of her next book, *Because You Matter: how to take ownership of your life so you can really live*, is planned for fall 2019. Connect with her on social media and at her website daniellebernock.com.

What There Is to Love About Michigan

Danielle Bernock

I was born and raised in Michigan. It's a beautiful state, and the only one with a *handy* map. You know someone's from Michigan when you see them in conversation pointing to a spot on their hand. That spot is where they live. I've met strangers by comparing my map with theirs. We feel a kindred bond. I thought I'd always live in Michigan. I was wrong.

Before the housing crash of 2008, my husband and I moved to Arizona. We lived there for about five years. Moving to a place you've never been before is life-changing in many ways. One thing I discovered was something Michigan had that Arizona didn't. Michigan has a vibrant color I love more than I knew.

Growing up in Michigan I'd taken this vibrant color for granted. It's everywhere, and I'd seen plenty of it, but red had always been my declared favorite color. I always loved how the trees put on a glorious display of reds and oranges in the fall. Arizona doesn't put on that display. I missed those colors in the fall when we lived there. But this other color? In Michigan it was too common for me to appreciate, until it was missing. I was guilty of the words in the old song by Joni Mitchell: *you don't know what you've got til it's gone.*

In Arizona, you could only find this Michigan color in

certain places. Not in my yard and not enough. You could find it in the more affluent communities. Places like Scottsdale and Fountain Hills. In these more affluent communities, the sprinklers kept this color alive. It took no small amount of water to keep the color from dying in the dry heat.

I lived in the little village of Laveen forty-five minutes away and had rocks for a lawn. Rocks don't need water. I learned to appreciate the rocks though. They didn't need any care. They were easy. But they didn't give off one of my favorite summer scents. I missed this color I hadn't known I loved.

When I visited my family in Michigan, I noticed something else. Something that didn't happen in Arizona. This color changes after a good rain in Michigan. All the vegetation takes on a luminous glow as if the vibrancy is singing for joy. In Arizona, it survives, breathing a sigh of relief that it will live another day.

When we moved back to Michigan, I knew I needed nature's carpet under my feet and its canopy above my head. We settled in Shelby Township, a community known for its trees. Our property is full of this vibrant color, and I know I love it now.

I have friends and family who *always* had this lush Michigan color as their favorite. Apparently, it's God's favorite too, because His throne is encircled with it. I didn't appreciate this vibrant color until I understood its value. This color speaks life. Arizona may have sunshine all year long, and I love sunshine. But something there is to love about Michigan is its display of life. Green is the color of life itself, and I love life.

.

Cynthia Anne Hurt

Cynthia Anne Hurt (CrowCAH) is currently editing her first full length novel. A pirate swashbuckler at heart, CrowCAH pillages the keyboard to write her novels, novellas, short stories, and poetry, while plundering the bookshelves for reading material. She is a member of the Sterling Heights Public Library Creative Writers Workshop and Romance Writers of America, plus the local Greater Detroit RWA chapter. Hurt has been a lifelong resident of Sterling Heights, Michigan. Contact her at cynthiaannehurt@gmail.com.

Dawning of a New Year

Cynthia Anne Hurt

The moment I walked in
though it be a sin
I saw your face
and set to a pace
straight towards your chair
without a care.

~ ~ ~

I sat, waiting for Sir Mykle to arrive at Queen Rosemont's "Dawning of a New Year" party on Sol Phairian Cloud Nine. My sight often travelled to the door.

He arrived very fashionably late, wearing a top hat and black tuxedo. His translucent white wings shone glossy.

Our eyes met.

I blushed.

"You do know," Sendall, my lady-in-waiting, whispered, "he's reported to be married."

"Hush. None of that." I slapped her fingers. "Just rumors." Snapping the fan open, I ushered air over my face and prayed to St. Bucyrus it wasn't true.

"As you say, my Lady." She rearranged my feathers to their greatest effect.

Straightening and fluttering my wings, I surveyed the splendor of the ballroom. The gilded glass walls revealed the sun's pure radiant rays and picturesque colossus clouds. Dawn had arrived. Inside gold chandeliers cascaded teardrop beads, showering the visitants with prisms.

"Excuse me, miss," he spoke, standing before me, "hear what I have to say before you dismiss."

Peering over my fan, I said, "Speak plain to me."

"I cannot conform to your request / I knew not this to be an inquest?"

"I do not dally with married men," I said, shuttering the fan closed.

He drew back. "Madam you must be remiss / for I have no mistress / nor wife / who can claim my strife."

"Can it be so?"

He nodded, "Lady Alana and I are divorced / it was all done in due course."

My mouth relaxed into a smile. "In that case, what have you to say?"

"I beg your leave / for your word and deed / to dance with me / do you agree?" He offered his palm.

I placed my hand in his and rose. "I do indeed."

He clasped my fingers and lead us to the dance floor. "May I offer you a compliment / it will only take but a moment?"

I waited with stilled wings.

"You look so lovely tonight / would you call me your Knight?"

"Sir Mykle, you are very polite. From this day you may carry this delight." I withdrew a handkerchief.

He grasped and kissed it, stuffing the trinket in his breast pocket. "I will treasure you for evermore / be it from this day or over four score."

"That's a long time, but with you by my side we shall require nothing more."

"I most certainly agree / a noble steed and me. Now, let us find a place where people will let us be."

Mykle led me to the balcony and stopped by the banister.
We kissed.

~ ~ ~

So you see my dear
there's nothing to fear
you're safely by my side
where nothing shall divide
unless one of us dies
then you'll be free to cry
but let us think of happier times
while I can still call you mine.

Widow's Walk

There I came to stand waiting
On the balcony
Of so many tomorrows

Squinting at the horizon
Lest I spot the clouds
Bearing my bold sailor home

Artist: Cynthia Anne Hurt

A Soul Owed

Cynthia Anne Hurt

Fog seeped through the timbers of *The Hound*, as it trundled its way over the waves on its destructive marked path.

For those who spied the fog knew the pirate DAGE, Devil Angel: Guardian of Eternity, was near.

~ ~ ~

DAGE peered through his telescope at the sailing frigate. His soot black wings quivered in anticipation of what was to come.

He espied a blonde-haired, petite woman on deck, clothed in trousers and a blouse. She offered weapons, which none of her crew took, and ran out the cannons all by herself.

They wouldn't do her any good. Not against one who couldn't die.

Since he received the written summons and the promise of a blood offering, his ship made quick time and soon overtook the slower vessel.

He had received numerous pleas for administering his charge on unsuspecting Human pirates who ran the gamut from petty theft to downright murder. Most cases were against captains, but few were ever women.

~ ~ ~

On the frigate, Sophie stopped her frenzied movements as she prepared the ship for battle. "Why ye all standin' like lubbers? Can't ye see the DAGE will soon be upon us?"

101

All the crewmen stared at her, their weapons laying where she put them. They were not even going to defend themselves.

From someone a low hum started, gaining intensity as it spread from person to person.

"Mutiny, is it?" Sophie fisted her hands. She had a feeling they would turn on her, but not so soon. There had to be more time. Glancing around at the men, she knew her hourglass had sprinkled all its sand.

The crew formed a horseshoe around her, leaving the railing as her only escape.

Whenever she neared a group of men, the closest ones would stop humming, while the others kept up their incessant buzz.

The only way to divert her mind from the inevitable was to keep busy. This was the life she had chosen. Nicholas had left her for his retirement on the mainland. He had never wanted to be a pirate, but his friend, Paul, had persuaded him and Sophie to enter the buccaneering profession.

"So be it," she huffed, priming the nearby cannons. The plan had to work. Or else...

She glanced at *The Hound*, the fog curling around the ship, creating its own cascading waves, and determined her fate was still a mile off. Sophie growled, holding her cutlass at the ready. "He'll see to it you all pay for your treachery." She knew her fight was not with the men, but the Devil Angel. The Fallen Sol Phairian Angel who went rogue, terrorizing the Earth with his superior speed and deathly grace.

Sophie ignited the slowmatch, discharging a cannon ball, which fell short of its target.

A warning.

~ ~ ~

DAGE closed the telescope, handing it to his quartermaster. "It's time."

"Aye aye, capt'n," the quartermaster said, barking out,

102

"furl the sheets, drop the drag anchor, prepare to board."

The Hound slid alongside the frigate.

The Fallen Angel crew vaulted across and landed nimbly on the ship's deck. They stood behind the Human men, guarding them.

~ ~ ~

To Sophie, *The Hound's* crew were lean and burly. Their pallor was corpselike, ashen gray, as if they never saw the sun. Yet their angular faces were strikingly beautiful, featuring soulful eyes which peered at her when she chanced to meet their gaze. It must have been a trick of the bright sunlight, but she could have sworn these creatures sprouted coal colored, translucent wings.

Boots thudded on her deck.

She spun, shaking her head, and focused on the swirling fog creeping towards her.

The mutinous buzzing from the crewmen ceased.

Appearing out of the condensed water was a tall, well-muscled man, who, despite his similar visage to the ghostly men, looked to be older and wiser. He had a panther-like, slow measured stride as he stalked toward her. His pale blue eyes radiated squint lines from working out in the sun. And there was no mistaking it this time, upon making eye contact, the DAGE's opaque, black wings became visible to her.

She started, but didn't back away, instead followed his movements, clenching her hand around the hilt of the cutlass not daring to use it—yet.

"You know of me?" the DAGE intoned, addressing Sophie.

The man's voice was smooth, like a reflective lake without ripples.

"I know of your purpose," she said.

He nodded. "Then you know I carry the Black Spot with me; a stain upon my very black heart."

Sophie swallowed. "I have acted honorably."

"There are those among us who would think otherwise."

She flicked her glance around the circled men. "They're a sorry lot of sea dogs. Turning me in with their tails betwixt their legs. Whining for praise from their dead master."

"Careful." Paul, Sophie's quartermaster, stepped forward.

DAGE flicked his graphite whip, scissoring between the pair and leaving mineral flakes and trace lines in its wake.

Paul stepped back. "Sophie, you erred when you refused to attack those enemy ships. How was I to appease the crew?"

"I did no such thing," she snarled. "If ye hadn't acted on your own, we wouldn't be in this mess now."

"I did it for the good of all," Paul spat.

"It seems," said DAGE, "that we are at the chasm of the future." He paced around the circle, making eye contact with all of the sailors and resting on Paul. "I have been promised a blood sacrifice."

Paul gulped. "It's not me."

"How can you be so sure?" DAGE settled his focus on Sophie. "It is for the one who receives the Black Spot to decide." Advancing, he said, "It's time for you to receive your mark."

Sophie retreated a few steps, extracting her cutlass.

The whip flashed out across the deck, wrenching the weapon out of her hand.

Clattering, the blade skittered to a halt near the bulwarks.

No one moved to retrieve it.

She stilled and glanced at Paul. "I'm not the problem, he is."

"He will get his due in time," DAGE stood in front of Sophie, holding out his right hand.

It looked inconspicuous, normal enough: four fingers, a thumb, and a palm. All except for the perfect circle mark on the back of his hand.

"Shake it, girl."

Sophie blinked, making no movement.

The whip twitched, coiling at its master's feet.

She shook her head. "If I refuse?"

"You give him the satisfaction he has wanted for some time."

"And if I do?"

"A slow death."

DAGE smiled, enjoying that either alternative she chose resulted in death, his forte.

The former would be by him and quick—the person's soul joining the fog, ushering the ship forward.

The latter would be by the person who received the Black Spot. That person either could chose to live as a Human, knowing they killed the one who summoned him, but would also be at the DAGE's beck and call. Or they could live for eternity, slowly becoming a Fallen Angel, choosing life aboard *The Hound* with him for forever—a personal death by their own hand.

Either way, he received an aura to add to the fog of souls or a human body to join the crew. For as long as he was needed to dispense the Black Spot, there would always be persons with greed, and greed fed his crew with ample manna to continue their deathly service.

He gripped the whip's handle and wriggled his wrist, causing the tendril to writhe and flop on deck like a fish out of water.

Sophie clasped his cold and bony hand.

DAGE squeezed hers, causing the beauty mark to enlarge, blistering at the edges as the skin stretched and allowed the shiny silver mitt to plate out like armor and cover his hand and that of Sophie's.

She gasped and tried to retract, but already the metal fist had entrapped it, forcing tiny needles to tap into her skin.

It took all of a few minutes before the pain stopped, the pressure eased, and DAGE's hand morphed back to normalcy.

Sophie was a marked woman.

"You still have yet to make your decision," DAGE said, striding to the center of the group.

She ran her finger over the doubloon sized black tattoo and noticed her skin was smooth, no raised bumps signaling fresh ink.

"Well?" DAGE flicked the whip, sending it zipping out and striking the deck, a sooty line radiating out from where he stood.

She focused on the true enemy. Not her crew mates, but the fiend himself. Why had she come up with this plan? It seemed foolproof when they talked about it, but the execution was another thing. "It seems I have little choice in the matter."

"I'm owed a soul. I care not for whose it be, whether the one carrying the spot or the one who summoned me. For if not, I can enlist your services when the need arises. A flotilla at my command."

"I will not be your puppet."

"Your choice is made? You will kill the one who paid for my services in blood money?" He smiled.

Paul took another step into the circle. "That wasn't part of our agreement."

One of the DAGE's crew restrained Paul by the shoulder.

"Or," continued DAGE, "you can symbolically kill yourself by joining me on *The Hound*, sailing out the rest of your eternal days."

"Never!" Sophie tore a knife from her boot and flung it at DAGE.

His whip zipped through the air, deflecting the blade which embedded itself in Paul's heart.

She gasped, lurching towards her friend, who remained standing only by the clutch of his restrainer.

Her crew collectively became animated only to be

thwarted by the Fallen Angels holding them back.

Paul stared first at DAGE, then focused on Sophie. A single tear streamed down his cheek.

The guard released his grip.

Paul collapsed to the deck.

"That was not my choice," Sophie indicated the fallen man.

"You didn't make a decision, so I did, adding to my collection." DAGE's eyes glinted. "Throw him over."

Two Angels hoisted the body and flung it over the rail. The ensuing splash broke the silence.

Holding up her hand, she said, "I still have the mark."

"And there it shall remain until you decide whose life is more valuable, your own or the mutineer's?"

"What?" Sophie searched the circle of men, trying to make sense of what just happened. Paul wasn't the only one to summon the DAGE.

She staggered and leaned upon a cannon.

It was herself.

Sophie and Paul had cavorted together and orchestrated the plan. He was to take the responsibility, but she was the sole mastermind. Summon the DAGE, receive the Black Spot, and cause terror to their enemies. How had the crew known of her treachery? They didn't advertise their mission. But even she, too, had felt the DAGE's growing attraction, ever since they sent the summons, with every gust of wind that brought him closer. She shuddered at the knowledge of what her folly had wrought.

He stood before her, gloating.

How could he be so cruel to ask this decision of her? Join his armada or die herself to living memory?

Sophie straightened. "I'm ready."

"What will it be?" DAGE's toothy smile gleamed in the filtered sunlight.

"I'm joining him." She pulled a knife from her bodice and

thrust it into her abdomen.

DAGE's whip struck out, snapping in the air and slithering useless to the deck.

Crumpling to her knees, Sophie extracted the bloodied knife and watched as her life ebbed from her veins, moistening the deck around her. She lifted her head, smirking, "Not yours."

"Infernal woman!" DAGE thundered. He couldn't be satisfied with this outcome, not when he wanted to relish making her last living days a nightmarish hell as she sailed the seas with him. He had wanted her for himself, admiring her from afar and praising her skill as a Human pirate. Now she was dead to him, no longer within his power. She had thwarted him, even till the end.

He advanced upon Sophie's prone form. Crouching, he gazed into her sightless eyes. "Goodbye, my love." Shutting her eyes, he lifted her in his arms. Flying over to *The Hound*, he ordered, "Make sail."

His crew obeyed their leader, transferring ships, and leaving the frigate behind.

If the DAGE could not have Sophie physically as a partner, he sure as hell was going to consume her soul spiritually. Her essence would guide him eternally on his gruesome business.

Loretta Sponsler

Loretta Sponsler has a degree in journalism. She has worked in marketing, public affairs, technical writing, and content creation. Today, she spends her time raising three boys and attempting to write children's books. She enjoys gardening, hiking, and starting projects that she never finishes, including writing various books.

The Plight of the Beloved Critic

Loretta Sponsler

"Honey, do you need this list?" I ask. "It says milk, eggs, packing tape…and I think there is a song or a poem."

"I don't remember writing that," she says.

"It's your handwriting. It says, quote, 'And my teeth sink softly in your skin, and I can taste all the places that you've been,' end quote. Kinda dark, Jane," I joke. "Did you get the milk?" Why do I even bother asking about something as practical as milk?

She takes the paper and walks away. Obsessed in an instant.

She won't come to bed tonight. Her fingers will bang the keyboard in a manic struggle to capture the story. Trap the idea before it escapes. Or derails. Or dies on the long road from what is imagined to what is real. "Real" on paper anyway.

She will ask me to read her story. My opinions. Any changes, suggestions I might have. Around here, the husband gets the first drafts. And, I will read it…fool that I am.

"The story seems to go flat in the middle," I say. "I think it needs more dialogue. Show, don't tell…right, Jane?"

Self-righteous rage glares back at me. How dare I criticize? The one who never builds but only destroys. Me, the killer of dreams and assassin of creations. Her accusations, never spoken out loud but spoken all the same.

After all, no one *really* likes a critic. She won't come to bed tonight either.

My role is to plant the seeds. Doubt will grow. Acceptance, given enough time. Edits will be made. Revision after revision. A never-ending process.

She will grow closer to her characters as she drifts further from me. I will watch her excitement turn to self-doubt. Her dedication turn to self-loathing.

At some point, she will throw it all away. Abandon the whole story, both from her mind and her heart. That's when I will get my wife back, the one who laughs at my jokes and comes to bed at night. A brief lull in the mania, a brief pause before her characters call her back once more.

It seems to me, giving birth to a novel is a lot like giving birth to a child. I was witness to that, as well. It was also a long process, full of agony and tears and a remarkable amount of swearing. Children are born, as are books, and the labor is cruel and all-consuming.

The ends justify the brutal means. A child. A novel.

Others see the before, the after…but I bear the scars of the in-between.

AF Jerzowski

AF Jerzowski, writer and dog lover, will be publishing her first book soon. It is about a dog she adopted from her vet, the owner of Serenity Animal Hospital. Serenity is actively involved in dog rescue efforts. She applauds the efforts of serious, careful, and dedicated rescue organizations. Through her writing she intends to highlight those efforts.

Willie and Max

AF Jerzowski

My best friend's name is Max. He's a black and white dog, and he's scared of humans. My name is Willie. From what I can see when I lick my paws and other stuff, I'm a red-brown color, and I try to protect Max. For that, I get hit by the human I call Big Guy.

Max and me lived in the same small crates all our lives. All our lives with humans we didn't like. Big Guy and his buddy, Mean Lady.

Today everything changed. Big Guy and his buddy took us in a van to a place. I didn't see Mean Lady's fly swatter anywhere, so I figured Max and me were safe from her. They carried us from the van to a building and handed us over to a guy wearing a jacket. He took us and held us both, up in the air, one under each arm. I wasn't sorry to see the back of Big Guy walking away. Mean Lady stood in front of us and Jacket Person. She said, "You two are being retired."

She changed her voice to talk to Jacket Person. "Be quick about it."

"They won't see it coming," he said.

She turned and walked to the van. Jacket Person closed the door with his foot and took us to a "go potty" place. We ended up in a crate together with some food and water.

"Hey, Max, this is different." I was pretty sure Max knew I

meant that we were in the same crate, instead of two crates next to each other, like we were used to.

Max said, "I want more food, Willie."

"Maybe he'll bring more later."

We tried to settle down. The smells in this place hit my nose kinda hard. Lots of different dog smells almost covered something I never smelled before. Me and Max looked at each other and wiggled our snouts. The stink of the van that brought us here still sat in my nose—and now we had to get used to new stink.

A human took our food bowl away. She patted me on my head and tried to pat Max, but he backed into a corner with his ears and tail down. She turned her head this way and that like she was looking for someone, and the tail on top of her head bobbed with her. She said, "You look like Papillons, maybe mixed with Dachshunds? So cute."

Her scent floated around her, and her voice made my tail wag. She leaned into us and her tail bobbed forward on one side of her face. I decided I would call her Tail Head. In a quiet voice, she said, "I'm going to try to spring you two."

I wagged my tail more to show her I was a good boy. She seemed happy to meet us, more like a dog would be than a human.

Jacket Person walked back in the room, and I felt Tail Head stiffen. I looked at Max and said, "Do you think Jacket Person knows she's afraid of him?"

"When are they scheduled?" she asked as she stood up from our crate after closing our door.

"Sooner the better. Don't want to have to feed them for too long. I think probably tomorrow night after the last batch comes in for the week." Jacket Person spoke matter-of-factly like he didn't care one way or the other. Tail Head seemed tense but alert. *Too bad this guy takes her "happy" away.*

I watched the guy with the jacket walk out of the room. Tail Head followed him, but not before she looked back at me and Max.

"Did you see her smile at us, Max?"

After a while, Jacket Person came back and took us out. We did our business while the sky was getting dark. Back in our crate, we curled next to each other to sleep. Other dogs in the building had stopped barking and whining, so we knew the humans left us alone for the night.

We woke up hearing noises from outside. Max, me, and other dogs behind the walls started barking. Max whimpered.

The light switched on in our room as Tail Head walked in with two other humans. *Why is everyone smiling?* I wagged my tail. Max backed into the corner of the crate.

"Aren't you the pretty boys?" A new human with long fingers talked while trying to pat us. She had to stretch those fingers to get to Max. His tail stayed down.

"Can you believe they want to get rid of these two sweet Papillons?" said Tail Head.

"Beautiful mixed breeds," said Long Fingers.

"Papillons are housed with Dachshunds at that puppy mill," Tail Head said while pulling us out of our crate.

The third human in the room, the one right behind Long Fingers, said, "They'll be even more beautiful after a bath." She wrinkled her nose. A name to call her did not come to me right away. She opened her mouth when she smiled and I saw a big space between her teeth. I decided to call her "Toothless."

I found myself wrapped up in Long Finger's arms.

Max peed on Toothless when Tail Head handed him over to her. "Oh no," Toothless said, holding Max away from her body. Tail Head wiped her pant leg with a rag.

I looked at Max and wondered why he marked Toothless. Obviously, Long Fingers was the Leader of the Pack. I decided to stick with Long Fingers. I would never mark her.

We were in another van, riding with Long Fingers and Toothless. The pee and poop smell was covered over with a scent that did not bother me. The humans talked. "Can you believe they kill their breeders?"

"Common practice. Sad, but true. Puppy mills decide they've outlived their usefulness. No searching for a forever home, just dispose of them. Ship them to a place with a high kill rate."

Max and me were so tired we barely noticed the stops to pick up other dogs. We slept and slept.

After a long ride, the humans emptied us out of the van. Long Fingers handed us over to a girl who smelled like treats. Max and me liked her and especially her right side pocket with the treats in it.

We got crates next to each other, clean water, good-tasting kibble, and a soft blanket to push around and sleep on.

"Hey, Max, I like this blanket thing."

Max didn't talk and I saw he was already sleeping.

In the morning, Treat Pocket came for Max. I watched him get carried away. Someone else came to take me to potty. Just as I scooted back into my crate, Treat Pocket brought Max back. She frowned as she said, "Sorry, Maxie, maybe next time." She kissed him and gave him a treat.

I had my eyes on that right pocket when she came for me. "Let's see if they like you, Willie." She smiled as she let me smell her now-empty pocket. We went through a door and she placed me on the floor. I could smell that Max had peed in several spots in this room.

Long Fingers sat on a big rug; Treat Pocket was behind me; a lady with a big smile sat on the other end of the rug; another lady sat on a bench.

I ran past Long Fingers, straight to Smiley Lady. I liked the way her smile made her eyes sparkle and scrunch up. Sitting down in front of her, between her two legs, made her laugh. She said something. Don't know what she said, but her voice was soft and felt good in my ears. I decided to stay.

Long Fingers looked happy when she said, "What do you

think?"

Lady on the Bench said, "He's a cutie, and he didn't pee on everything like that poor Max."

Treat Pocket said, "His name is Willie. Isn't his coat a rich mahogany color?"

Lady on the Bench noticed his crooked front paw. "What happened to his foot?"

Long Fingers said, "He might have been born that way, but we'll never know for sure."

I could tell Smiley Lady had a sadness deep inside her. *Maybe she needs a friend?* She talked, and I thought, *I don't know what she's saying, but it all sounds good.*

She said, "My mother suggested a name and I think it fits Willie a little better. He doesn't look like a Willie to me."

Everybody got quiet. Smiley Lady looked right in my eyes and announced, "I think I'll call him Sparky."

I let out one quick bark and wagged my tail.

Mark Morgan, Jr.

Mark Morgan, Jr. is a Detroit native, teacher, and poet. He enjoys meetings with the Poetry Workshop in Saint Clair Shores and the Creative Writers Workshop in Sterling Heights.

His work is featured in the 2018 edition of *Sterling Script: A Local Author Collection* and by *The Rising Phoenix Review*. Mark also won Landmark Books' Fourth Annual Haiku Contest in 2018. When not writing or teaching, Morgan may be found reading, practicing martial arts, or listening to jazz.

Frostbitten Wings

Mark Morgan, Jr.

at some precise moment
the universe may permit
you to sit back and watch
a Michigan winter squirm
out from its chrysalis
and flutter its veiny wings
against your windshield. but
no time will be wasted—one
snowflake's desperate tumble
equals a thousand weddings
ten billion funerals
and one mediocre job
interview. you may leave
the office shivering or
thirsty for sweet streetlight
nectar. who hasn't denied
their entire existence
is a trajectory through
a blizzard of questions?
only when frostbitten wings
grow silent do skies turn clear

Swallowtail

Mark Morgan, Jr.

```
Swallows
        dart
  through
        the
        sky,
                                      their    k
                                        for   ed
                                                    tails
                                              beh
                                      ind
                                            them

              as
          they
  zi                                          b
    g                                           r
    -z                            t  h  r   o   u  g  h
      ag                                      k
                                                e
                                                n

                    ws
        o               andch          f
      d                     a  nl  nk   e
      n                        i   i    n
        i                               c
          w                             e
                                        s
                                    .

                            .

                          .

        I want to fly like that.
```

Shower

Mark Morgan, Jr.

If I could be anything
I would be the rain
so I could mix with your
perfume and sweat
trickle down your body
turn into honey on your lips
and keep you soaked
until your fingertips wrinkle.

Judith K. Smouter

Judith K. Smouter earned her Bachelor's Degree in Physical Education from Michigan State University and her Master's Degree in Exercise Physiology from Wayne State University. As a working professional, she was employed in a variety of positions including cardiac rehabilitation Exercise Specialist, self-employed exercise physiologist, K-9 physical education teacher and during the pinnacle of her career she became an Associate Vice Chancellor at Wayne County Community College District. Her love and dedication for sports helped her become a member of the US National Speed Skating Team from 1971-1975. Her hobbies include painting, traveling, and, more recently, writing. She is a wife and mother. She has two children and three grandchildren.

Yosef's Eternal Hopes and Dreams

Judith K. Smouter

May, 1940

"Alina, here it comes. You got it, now kick it back to me," I yelled.

With a mighty strike, the ball sailed in my direction, causing Alina to lose her balance and fall backwards. My eyes widened and my mouth fell open as I ran towards her.

Alina burst out laughing. "Wow, that was my best kick ever!"

I slid to the ground next to her, and we rolled over the earth and giggled uncontrollably.

September, 1941

As the two seven-year-old friends sat next to each other on the floor and leaned up against the wall of their crowded apartment, I reflected, "Alina, do you remember the time you kicked the soccer ball so hard you fell?"

"Yes, that was so funny. I miss playing soccer with you."

"We practiced every day after school," I interjected. "I still dream of becoming a great soccer player, maybe even making the Polish Olympic team."

Alina put her head down, and, with her voice saturated with sadness, she responded, "Everything changed. Now we are hungry all the time and don't have the energy to play."

I hugged her and whispered in her ear, "Things will get better. We must keep our hopes up."

That night, a loud hammering sounded on the door of our living quarters. Troubled, my papa opened it.

A man in uniform commanded, "Everyone here has been chosen to go to the land of milk and honey. Bring only your most important possessions and label your luggage, one bag per person. Be in front of your apartment in thirty minutes for transport." In military fashion, he turned and stomped away.

Papa shut the door and paused as he locked fearful eyes on Mama, then his gaze shifted to all the other families in the crowded room. Papa, designated leader of our group, told everyone to do as the officer instructed. With tears welling up in his eyes, he came over to where I was standing, knelt down and wrapped his arms around me.

"Go pack your clothes, son."

I was confused.

Why was everyone so sad? They all looked scared. We've moved before, but this move sounds like we are going to a better place. I thought. In the Torah, the land of milk and honey was the land promised by God. Maybe at this new settlement, we'll be fed better. I would love to taste milk and honey again. With new strength, I will be able to run fast and play soccer as I used to. That's what I will pray for.

Putting my prized soccer shoes on top of my clothes, I zipped up my bag. After Papa and Mama finished packing, we went outside along with everyone else in readiness to be picked up.

"The truck is coming!" cried Mama.

With a terrified look on her face, she insisted that I hold her hand. This made me a little scared, but I welcomed her loving touch.

Alina and her family stood next to ours.

"Maybe we can sit by each other on the truck," suggested

Alina.

"I hope so," I agreed.

The military truck stopped and soldiers jumped out. They proceeded to push and prod all the people into the back of the vehicle. Such uncalled for roughness by the soldiers provoked many to resist in protest while others simply cried.

I asked Mama, "Why were the soldiers so mean?"

"I don't know, my little man. I do know that we must be brave. Can you do that?"

"Yes, Mama."

After an hour of agonizing travel in the crammed full truck, we stopped. The back doors swung open, and we were told to unload quickly. Once everyone was out of the truck we were rushed over to a cattle car on a train track. As before, we were forcefully herded into the car. It was dark with the doors closed, making it hard to see so I tried to listen to everyone around me. Some were talking, others crying, but most were quiet probably in deep thought. After twenty minutes of standing still, the train began to move. Oh no, I suddenly felt the urge to pee.

I tugged on Mama's hand and said, "Mama, I need to go."

There were small cracks in the walls of the car letting in a little light, so our eyes had become accustomed to the darkness. Mama looked around and together we slowly made our way over to the corner of the car. I relieved myself and then we maneuvered our way back to Papa. After two miserable hours on the train, we arrived at our destination.

"Get out of the car," an official shouted. "Drop your luggage on the landing and go to the showers for disinfection. Your baggage will be returned to you later."

Soldiers pushed into the crowd and began to separate the men from the women and children. Papa held on tight to Mama and me when unexpectedly he was brutally knocked to the ground by a soldier's baton.

"Don't hurt my papa," I screamed as I kicked the soldier.

The soldier's face reddened and he raised his club over me. Instantly, Mama reacted and covered me saying, "He is very sorry, very sorry. We will do as you say."

The officer's rage subsided.

Mama looked at Papa's bloodied face. He looked back at her and nodded, signaling us to go.

Mama directed me to join the other women and children who were being coerced to the showers.

"Mama, is Papa going to be alright?" I whimpered.

"Yes, son. Be brave, remember?"

As we reached the showers, I felt a trembling hand on my shoulder. Alina was reaching out to me. As we looked at each other, we both said, "I love you."

The authorities told our group to take off our clothes and go into the shower. The shoving and intimidation by the officers were met with screams and wailing. Unable to resist any longer, our entire group was driven into the shower. We were packed in so tightly. As everyone was waiting for the water to come out of the shower heads, a gas misted out instead.

I coughed, "Mama, I don't feel good."

"It's okay, Yosef. Know that I love you with my whole heart." With tears trickling down her cheeks, she kissed me.

I struggled to talk, but with one last choked effort, I asked, "Mama, do you think I will be able to play soccer in the land of milk and honey?"

Jim Stone

Jim Stone, also known as poet Kalle Kivi, is a member of the Creative Writers Workshop and Shelby Writers. He's an author who enjoys traveling, gardening, and Michigan's four seasons. As a poet, he has performed at open mic events within the community.

Stone has written for the *Michigan Citizen*, the *Detroit River Current Newsletter*, and was a part of the writing team for the American Heritage Rivers Initiative for the Detroit River.

He is a graduate of the University of Michigan and Utica High School.

The Slide

Jim Stone

"Why, that can't be the doorbell, can it? Not at this hour, way past my bedtime," Mabel whispered to herself, half asleep. "I better get up and check, just in case it's some emergency where someone needs my help." Mabel Cooper lived her life to help other people, even perfect strangers, as she had been taught, by example, so long ago by her loving extended family.

Just as she swung her old bones out of bed, Mabel heard the front storm door rattle, as if someone was desperately trying to pull it open.

"Hold your horses, whoever you are, you know I must have been sleeping; and I'm not as quick as I used to be! I am coming."

Turning on the light switch from pure muscle memory, Mabel ambled slowly but steadily down the short hallway to a tidy living room. Christmas lights strung around the inside of her picture window framed a small ceramic Christmas tree on the table below. "Oh my," Mabel noticed, "We have a good snowstorm brewing, so the children will have a white Christmas! Us old people, too."

Mabel didn't remember grabbing her old gray and purple cardigan sweater. Besides this gift from her long departed dear sister—*Was it ten, or twenty years ago?*—she only had on her nightgown and house slippers as she approached the front door. She saw the porch light switch in the "on" position.

The sturdy oak door did not have a peephole, like her grandchildren kept bugging her to have put in. "Why bother," she would tell them, "When my Bill was alive we didn't need one, and now that he's gone, what, three years now, or has it been thirteen? In any event, I may be old, but I'm not feeble, and I can get along by myself just fine, why thank you, Jesus." Mabel unlocked the trusty deadbolt latch like so many thousand times and grabbed her walking cane from its place under the light switch before opening the door to have a look outside. "I hear the old north wind howling, and I ain't as steady as I once was. Hold on, whoever you are, I'm right here!" She spoke the latter aloud, with authority.

"Oreo! Oreo, you stinker; get back into this house this instant!" Mabel cried out to no avail as her black-and-white cat scampered outside between her ankles when she cracked open the outer door. *No mousing for you on this wintry night; they are smart enough to be nestled up in their sleeping places while this storm is blowing.* Stepping outside and seeing no-one, Mabel knew she had to go snatch the rascal, so she yelled into the wind, "Oreo...Oreo...Here kitty, kitty."

Mabel did not think of closing the inner oak door when the wind closed the storm door for her. With cane in her right hand, she grasped the porch rail in her left, and methodically counted her routine, "Step one, step two, sidewalk."

Her head-high, wire outdoor Christmas tree blinked red, green, and white in the front yard. She stopped to catch her breath and steady herself as she admired it. *Such memories,* she scrolled through past years in an instant. *How my dear Bill and I found it at one of those day-after-Christmas sales. How he showed me how to stake the circular base securely into the ground for windy nights like this. And how I still put it up this year, all by myself, with my good neighbors Phil and Sandy watching by; or was it Roger and Mary-Jo? No—they moved away; yes—we used to have such fun around Christmas.*

Now what am I doing out here? Mabel turned her eyes away from her cozy bungalow to the streetlight and the gusting, swirling snow. A stray plastic bag tumbled across the snow covered sidewalk two doors down. "Oreo! You stinker...bad kitty. I see you... Wait right there for mommy... I'm coming to getcha... Oreo."

At the intersection of her street and busier Fulton Avenue, Mabel focused on a spotlight from the elementary school in the distance. No cars were out at three in the morning. Laughing to herself as she kicked the snow with her house slippers, she said, "I see your tracks. I know your stomping grounds... Come, Oreo... Come to mommy. I have some tree—eats!" She felt them in her sweater pocket when she instinctively pulled it tight around her bony shoulders to ward off the elements.

Whoops! I must be careful on my walks. Where are Mr. and Mrs. Davis, my walking buddies from church? She quickly moved her cane forward to avoid a rut in the sidewalk, knowing it was down there somewhere, *Why doesn't someone fix the thing already; a kid walking to school can trip and skin his knee!* After two long blocks, she managed to reach the playground. A fence pole by an open gate was freezing cold to her bare hand. Mabel ignored the pain, but wobbled into the lonely space, regardless.

Four solitary swings chinkled as they bounced in the wintry gale. *I like the slide better,* Mabel recalled as she struggled toward it. The down part of the slide's chute was away from the wind, and by fate, away from Fulton Avenue. Before sitting down, she watched a lone truck, going to or from some night shift job, drive by carefully. The driver, mindful of the slippery potholed road, did not see her. Mabel jumped when her half exposed flesh touched the cold aluminum slide.

"Come on down now, you chicken," Mabel called up to her little sister Julie, "I'll either catch you here or come tickle you to death." Mabel only stopped giggling when she heard her teeth chattering. Reaching a shivering hand to her mouth to warm it on her breath, she remembered, *you wear dentures now, you silly girl; they must be back home by the sink...Oh Billy, Billy...you can't catch me...don't let your uncle find us kissing behind the barn...Mr. William Cooper, do you take Miss Mabel Dawson, to be your...I now pronounce you...*

Cold and exhausted, Mabel laid gently backward onto the slide, feet dangling free as her walking cane fell aside into the snow. An instant of lucidity swept over her when she fiercely gripped the cold rails in each shaking hand. *I've wandered off! Just like they all warned me. Ninety two and I passed my driver's license back in the spring. What a life I led! I love you all...I believe in God the Father, Almighty...*

Mabel did not remember releasing her grip on the slide's railings and folding tired, old arms tight across her chest. She glanced quickly from side to side, afraid, before relaxing and smiling into the misty distance. Her last conscious thought was the cross she saw amidst swirling snow, actually a telephone pole and wires next to the schoolyard. This gave her great comfort. *I believe in Jesus Christ...His only Son, our Lord...*

"It's me, Mabel, my dear. Billy's waiting for you... Bill Cooper... I'm back from the war... The children are packed in the station wagon with the beach gear... Keep wearing that pretty summer dress, and we'll have twins next time... Trust me, my dear... We'll be together soon." The voice was faint, but calming. Mabel felt its tone as she heard it. "You must see some other people first... It's just the way they do things up here... You will know..."

6th of July, 1992, Saturday Night

Jim Stone

That second phone call made my heart jump. Pop-pop-pop sounds of firecrackers down the block had escalated to the whee—boom sound of bottle-rockets. I knew the caller was my backyard neighbor Bill.

"Say, Sam," Bill mumbled before I could even say "hello." "Thanks for trying to quiet those idiots down, but it didn't work. If you listen, they seem to be starting up again from the same spot."

"Yeah, Bill, it's my neighbor Michelle's boyfriend, Joey, and his friend, Nitro. I know Joey a little bit and talked to them like you asked. Told them about your situation with fireworks and all. Michelle understands, but she has her hands full keeping three young kids up on the porch, and Joey told me 'five more minutes and we'll be done.' Sorry, I figured they got the message. Want me to call the cops?"

"Don't bother," Bill replied. "I'll come down and handle the situation personally. Don't want to have to, know what I mean? Thanks again, but one last favor, please, because I'm as scared as I am pissed off, you see…"

"What is it, Bill? I think I know where you're coming from. Anything I can do to help. Don't make things worse."

"Meet me there in the alley where they're shooting 'em off in five minutes. Don't tell anyone I'm coming out. Introduce me only as your neighbor, and let me do the talking. One more thing, most important, be my witness if I lose it and do something stupid. My girlfriend here is afraid to come out with me. You have my exes' and two kids' phone numbers, right? Just in case I get locked up for putting someone in the hospital."

Bill's last statements about losing it and family phone numbers made my skin creep. "Think it over, Bill. I'll be there when you talk—talk to them, but let me try one more time."

"Thanks, Sam, but no thanks. Don't like direct action at my own hands, but I have no other choice. I'm at wit's end. Meet me there and please remember this conversation in your witness statement to the cops. But don't call them now, okay? And no—I won't need you for back-up, just be there." Bill's calm detachment made my arm and neck hairs jump to attention. I hung up and started for the door.

"Sandra, you know the difference between fireworks and gunshots when you hear 'em, don't you?" I asked my girlfriend on the couch next to me.

Turning her head at an angle with one eyebrow raised, she whispered in her Jamaican accent, "White man, you crazy! I live this city all my life since little girl of ten. What you mean 'do I know difference?' Ha, ha, ha."

"Well, it looks like I have to go out mediate this situation. Bill from out back is coming around to confront those young guys blowing off fireworks. The man is legitimately what we call 'Card Carrying Crazy.' I'm a peacemaker, but I don't like this situation. So stay here and listen. Hear gunshots from close—call 911. Please."

"Okay, mon, but you remember I tell you my ex is Detroit Police, and they say, 'Around Fourth of July second best time of year next to New Year Eve Midnight to shoot someone with gun and get away with it,'" she reminded me. "Tell those young fools that before Bill gets his chance. Plus, this

Saturday night, mon. Too many shoot; not enough cars on street to respond. Ambulance what—half hour if lucky? You be careful yourself."

I didn't stop to relay that vital tidbit to Joey and Nitro as I ran past them into the alley. Another car had pulled in across the street from me (at least they had common sense enough to park away from the firing zone), and two more young guys I never seen before, twelve packs of beer in hand, had joined the party. I turned to the front porch to warn level-headed Michelle and her scatterbrained younger sister to get the kids into the house, please, before Bill shows up. At that moment, a colorful ground display goes off—all spinning, blasting and sparkling some ten feet high. Fallout was hitting the streets and lawn, and I wanted to make them stop, but looked down the alley for Bill before he "introduced himself."

"Hope that's water in the 5-gallon bucket, not kerosene!" I half-joked to Joey when I looked back at their display. He was putting out a small fire on the grass next to the alley.

"Good idea!" Joey shouted back. "Got some in the garage. Hey, want a cold brew?"

I waved him off as I went down the alley to meet my neighbor, "Wild Bill."

Bill stayed in the shadows by a privacy fence and some weed trees. I saw a shadow turn from his street into the alley. Street lights behind the main drag businesses flickered, adding to the tension. If I didn't know he was coming, I would have never noticed. He approached in fits and starts, crouching behind a bush as something else distant blew off. I noticed why he didn't just walk right up.

Dressed in black and green jungle camouflage from head to toe, Bill blended perfectly into the urban night environment. A canteen plus other packs hung from a thick belt at his sides. He wore no combat helmet, nor was he carrying any rifle I could see—*Thank you, Jesus*—only a well-worn baseball cap sporting the black helicopter silhouetted over green, red and yellow stripes. The word this image represented was not necessary: Vietnam.

Grabbing my T-shirt at the chest, Bill twisted it into his fist under my chin with the curve of his wrist. I felt bone pressure hard against my windpipe as he pulled me down to my knees next to him, crouched on one knee. Face streaked with black and green camo paint, he addressed me sternly, "Always identify yourself as a friendly with a whistle or hand signal next time. Things change too fast here in the field. I couldn't know positive it was you; streetlight behind puts your face and body in shadow, plus light blindness in my eyes."

"Sorry, sir," I whispered, gasping to get back my breath. "Lieutenant, won't happen again. Sam of Newcastle Street Squad reporting for duty, sir. And you can take your boot off my ankle now—I only have sandals on." Bill's polished combat, work boots were steel toed and shanked. I knew there'd be a visible bruise and welt tomorrow; I took the pain for now. *Holy Moly,* I pondered. *Why can't a guy have a quiet night with his lady?*

"Take point," Bill ordered after finally releasing me. "Say nothing about me at first, only name introductions. Let me do the real negotiating, none of your psycho-babble. Keep your eyes on me at all times as you scan and assess the enemy's strength vs. weakness. I'll nod and touch my cap when I need you to step in. And don't call me Lieutenant, dammit! I body bagged and med evacked too many of those sorry book-learners for my taste—brings back bad memories, bad karma. This mission is too important. Now move out!"

Approaching the scene, I saw two young women had joined the two strangers, my friend Joey, and his buddy Nitro.

"Make small talk first," Bill whispered hiding behind me close where I felt his breath at my neck. At the last minute he stepped to my side, showing himself to the others.

"About that beer, Joey?" I asked. "Send out two; this is my

backyard neighbor, Bill. Bring your buddies over for intros all around. Happy Fourth, everyone!" I said this greeting reluctantly, knowing why we joined in late.

One of the strangers tossed us the two beers and shouted as he saw Bill dressed in combat gear. "Dude—this is the Fourth of July, not Halloween! Nice Rambo look." In typical a-hole fashion, he said, "Let's light off some big ones."

Taking his beer and turning it slowly in his left hand so the bottom of the can is up, Bill winced at the label as if it is some muddy water from the Mekong swamps. He said nothing in response to the taunts. My mind blanked out, not even a "thank you" for the beers; I stood aside as Bill scanned the circle of people with eyes only, body tensed for some reaction, how severe I cannot predict.

With all eyes on him, waiting for some response to the Halloween comment, Bill flicked his right hand across his body and unsheathed an eight inch knife. Ignoring a "yup, it's Rambo" comment from the young woman, he used the knife to deftly poke and twist open a hole in the bottom of his beer can, then raised it to his lips before pulling the tab open from above, all the while holding his knife. In what seemed like one motion and half a second, Bill took the now empty shot-gunned beer can and dropped it from eye level. With dramatic effect, he sliced the can in two with an expert swipe of his razor sharp blade and stabbed one of the halves with the point before it hit the ground. He held it aloft for all to see. The cut is clean. The other half he stomped flat.

The four other young men followed my lead and gave Bill some space. There was laughter and cheers, despite the tension.

"Damn," I heard Joey shout in admiration before offering me a high-five, which I declined.

"Nope, you're not setting off any more, big ones or baby ones. Sorry, but the party's over," Bill announced in a clear voice barely louder than a whisper. He held up his wrist watch, pointing to it with his knife, "The time is twenty-three fifteen, quarter after eleven to you airheads who can't tell proper time. Pack it up and take it over to Balduck Park if you want...but it's definitely over...here. Now." The last word came loud as a command order.

Nitro and the other two young guys took defensive type motions to position themselves and surrounded Bill on three sides, away from Joey and me. The women stepped back. Bill said nothing more as he sheathed his knife after wiping the blade across a leather patch sewn on his outer pant leg. I gave Joey that look: "we better do something—quick," when he broke the tension and offered, "Good idea, huh, everyone? Nitro? De Dee? The big ones will look better up against the night sky; it will be safer and hey—we are getting pretty loud and someone might call the cops. I did promise we'd stop before you guys came. Balduck is only fifteen minutes."

"No one's callin' the cops, and anywho it's Saturday night of our long party weekend," one of the young ladies replied, catching her balance. "They won't come for just firecrackers, and you know that, Joey. You've lived here about a year now, right?" Turning to Bill, she said, "And who are you, granpaw, the neighborhood watch freak? You can't tell any of us what we can't do! It won't take the three of these here guys to kick your ass..."

Before her drawn out slurred 's' finished, Bill's knife whished end-over-end past her side and sticks, point first and perfect chest high, into the wooden telephone pole where the alley and sidewalk meet.

"Michelle, get those kids in the house; now!" Joey shouted up to the front porch. "C'mon guys, it ain't worth it. Is it, Sam?"

Noticing one of the guys patting his pants pocket, implying that he's got a gun and is not afraid to use it, I said, "No, it's not worth it. Go up to Balduck and blast away; better all round for everybody. Nobody wants trouble."

140

Just as I think the situation has calmed, the biggest of the young guys piped up, "We'll go, but not just yet." He pointed directly at Bill after stepping closer, "First you and me, pops. Backyard. No weapons—leave your knife in the pole, and my buddy will keep his gun in his pants. You come over here dressed to fight, so I'm calling your bluff. I say let's go. Michelle and Joey got that privacy fence. No neighbors, no cops, just us. Whaddya say?"

Bill made no move for his knife-stuck-in-the-pole or any other weapon hidden on his body. He showed no fear in his posture; no visible reaction to the young tough's challenge. The rest of us did show it, the quiet before the storm. Bill calmly held his hands to his sides, palms up, voice steady, "Everything is cool with me. Happy Fourth of July; red white and blue. But like I said before—this fireworks party is over. Some people, like me, just can't handle too much sound too close. So before we all go on our way; first let us drink a toast to old friends and new."

With one palm now held up at shoulder height, body language neutral but cautious, Bill asked me, "Sam, get that bottle out of my right leg pocket midway down. You all see my hands here in the air. Yes, the one that's zipped—she's not booby-trapped." Producing a fifth of Jack Daniel's Tennessee Whiskey, seal cracked, two healthy swigs gone, Bill said, "Thanks, brother," as I handed him the J.D.

The big guy went over to his mouthy girlfriend and told her to "Shut up or I'll...looks like Rambo here is goin' to pass it 'round. Toasts and stuff—before we go backyard." Joey nervously stepped over, shook Bill's hand and apologized, "Sorry, man. We should have shut the fireworks down after ten minutes or so. These guys, my old buddies, showed up with more stuff, and I wasn't sure if they were comin' or not."

"Accepted, new brother Joey," Bill replied. "But first before we drink—libations! To honor those no longer with us. Mitchell Johnson; Selma, Alabama; February 1967." He poured a quick shot of precious Jack onto some still hot debris that flashed briefly before dying out. Three more names, home towns, and dates of death up to May 1968 are poured before Bill tilts the bottle above his head to put the whiskey down. The once tense crowd is now diffused to Bill's liking, so he strode over to the man who challenged him to fight, handed him the bottle of Jack Daniel to the surprise of all. "Drink your fill, but say libations first." This is said as advice, not as an order.

The six-foot three-inch muscle-toned man in a white tank top took the bottle from the five-foot eight-inch skinny wisp of a man twenty some years his senior. He can now see close to read the patches sewn onto Bill's chest. U.S. Army. Rangers. 101st Airborne. Wild Bill. Raising the bottle and holding it out for all to see, he hesitated while holding back tears, "To Iron Mike, my older brother. East Side Detroit; August 25th, 1985. Shot dead protecting his lady and that dear little girl in the house—may I find the scumbag before the cops ever do."

Bill in turn took the bottle, turned his back to the big guy now wiping his eyes with his bare arm, personally handing it to everyone in the now closed circle, even the tipsy girlfriend, before finishing with me. He took great care to solemnly remind each person to pour a libation *before* drinking to someone's memory.

There were about four fingers of the fifth left when I held it up to the streetlight. Time seemed to stand still as I thought of whom to pour a libation to. Sound explosions echoed all around us from neighboring street-parties. Very few cars were moving on the main avenue or side streets. Bill didn't flinch at the occasional loud boomer going off, but I knew he was hurting inside—nerves and spirit. Buried memories brought out to simmer.

With that thought I was jolted out of a sudden reverie, a

hesitation that caused all but Bill to shout, "Go, go, go! Kill it, Sam, kill it. Don't be a wuss!" So I poured my libation toast onto the hard cement with great pride, looking neighbor veteran Bill straight into his bloodshot eyes, "To Charlie Jones, my father, still kicking and raising hell at 82. Proud World War II vet; Prisoner of War in German Occupied France; Purple Heart and Bronze Star. One tough SOB."

When I killed the JD to cheers all around, I was going to foolishly bust the bottle on the alley sidewalk with all the fireworks debris. Bill came out of nowhere to smartly grab it from me before I had the chance. "Take the empty to your dad next time you visit. Tell him about tonight, about our little ceremony. Be sure to buy him a fifth of his favorite (*Crown Royal, I knew from experience*) and thank him personally on my behalf for his service to our country." Bill loudly declared this last phrase at the young toughs and their girlfriends.

"Come on, people, one more big blaster before we go to Balduck," Nitro offered. "Especially after the toasts and stuff. Forget about fightin'; maybe some other time. 'Cause I got another fifth in the house I'll bring."

"Put that lighter away, pal, you just don't get it," Bill replied in his tired, detached voice that frightened me. Touching his cap, he handed me a plastic card from his shirt pocket. "Read this, Sam, loud enough for all to hear; but do it at my signal." I knew that Bill, playing it cool, was keeping a close eye on the three young guys.

"Yeah! Grand finale, grand finale," came the response from the three tanked up girls leading the chant. "Bring that last box over here in the middle of the street; ain't no cars coming. I ain't afraid to light it!"

Just as the big guy stooped down to reach for the fuse, the night was shattered by the deepest yet booming explosion in the distance. This one must have been of military grade, demolition, or mining quality, felt deep in your bowels and internal organs before the sound reached any ears. Everybody jumped as one. Car and house alarms erupted in sequence. We saw neighbors now come out to look about, curious, concerned.

As we gathered our wits about us, we didn't see Bill. No one noticed him scurrying toward Joey's driveway and diving under the nearest SUV. Laughs turned to silence as he carefully crawled out and dusted himself off. Crouching, tense, turning in a circle to alertly scout and assess the situation, Bill snatched his ID card from my hand.

"Listen, you all," he began as the noise seemed to die down. In a more nervous, vulnerable tone, "William T. McAllen; born April 4th, 1947. This card issued by VA Hospital, Allen Park, Michigan. It says in big letters here 'Psychiatric Unit. Priority One.' It is signed by Dr. Arthur P. Landis, MD. and Colonel Joseph Adam Gillette, MD. Vietnam Veteran. Honorable Discharge—August 24, 1968. US Army. In red letters, and I emphasize this last part for all smart asses out here: Do Not Restrain. Do Not Detain. Emergency 24 hour Hotline Call…"

"Big whoop," Nitro shot back. I never liked this buddy of Joey's from the get go, but even I was starting to get pissed when he added, "Are we having a Grand Finale right now or what!" Nitro waved his lighter, flame on.

Before I could step in to cool things off (or get my own ass kicked), Bill cried out in his resigned, tin voice, "Sam's daddy and your own grandpas came home to parades, ticker tape, bands playin' and all. When those of us lucky enough, or unlucky, came back home from The 'Nam we got cussed at, spit on, had bags of blood and piss thrown at us. I am a card carrying crazy, and I'm not going to jail when they take numbnuts here away in the ambulance if he or all of you jump me. Here's your 'Grand Finale.'"

Quick as Bill stashed his ID back into his shirt pocket, he pulled out a semi-automatic pistol from the small of his back.

144

Holding the barrel straight up to the night sky, he racked in a clip and told us, "The safety is off; I'm locked and loaded. Don't really care what happens now that I pulled this for all to see. Go ahead and try lighting off that last box in my face. The real grand finale will come when red lights flashin' come to drag your corpse away to the morgue, while the cops take me to the VA Hospital, not the Wayne County Jail. Trust me—the insanity defense will hold up in court. Bet none of you young punks ever thought about making out a will. Mine is on file; I've been ready to die for years now, and my conscience is clean."

"Go, you guys, I'll clean up," Joey shouted from where he was edging toward his porch.

"Thank God, a voice of reason," I whispered, out of earshot of Bill. "Please, Joey, don't call the cops. I'll walk Bill home. Please take the fireworks to Balduck Park or save them for next year."

That last box of the big fireworks went back into the car's trunk. I sensed that the mood was broken for any more light shows and boom-booms. Bill had lowered his weapon, barrel to the ground, safety on. He backed away toward the alley, eyes on alert. The crowd, one by one, followed Joey up onto his front porch and through the door. Nitro, the jerk, ever brave away from danger, yelled back, "Get some help, dude!"

Joey, the last one through the door, muttered, "Thanks" with a thumbs up. I returned the gesture and it was over.

"Jones, you dropped your weapon; stupid greenhorn!" Bill's voice the firmness of command again as he handed me an arm-size stick off the ground. "I'll take point; you cover our rear as we retreat. Quietly. Two clicks ahead and we'll switch positions on my hand signal. Keep alert."

Some hundred yards down the alley away from our encounter, we turned onto Bill's street. Ducking behind the large trees when a car passed from down the block, we crept low to the bushes in fits and starts until we reached Bill's house. Waving me to follow, Bill sprang through the unlocked front door. Once inside, he pointed to the stairs leading to the basement. "I'll bunker down; you keep watch," he ordered. I saluted back, stick-gun in hand.

Sneaking over to a phone on a desk, I was fortunate that rational Bill had left the VA crisis hotline phone number in laminated plastic taped to the wall. His new girlfriend, I had never met this one, crept down the stairs, pale as the moon.

After telling her I'm Sam, their backyard neighbor, she whispered, terrified, "Is he all right? I have never seen him this bad before, and I'm afraid to go down there with him right now."

"Good idea, do not," I replied. "No, he is not all right, and won't be for the rest of tonight. I am scared, too, so I'm going to stick my neck out and make that call. The crisis line will be super busy tonight, 4th of July weekend and all, but when I give witness to what just happened they should send someone out, priority. Could you please make some coffee? I'm going to sit up here and wait; someone with experience needs to come out to talk him down. No, do not go down with him just yet; he's really spooked. And no, I am not abandoning my post."

Fix the Engineers and Contractors
(our roads are fine)

An out-of-line sonnet - - - - - - -

Kalle Kivi

Cement is a mixture of water, sand, and lime
Asphalt a mixture of crushed rock, tar, petrol products
Momma always taught oil and water don't mix
So why use hot patch for cement pothole fix?

Michiganders love our four seasons
Football/hunting, winter, pothole, construction
Roll out the orange barrels—a driver's barrel of fun
Work may go slow, let overtime pay flow, job will someday
get done

Water finds ways into cracks above, into subsurface below
Freeze-thaw cycle teasing, washboard roads increasing
All dictated by laws of physics and chemistry
Subject to human trial and error fallacy

Overloaded semi, miles per hour, hits pothole with power
Cement chunks work loose, asphalt lanes form grooves
Snow plow salt truck knocks rocks and patches unstuck
Driver swerves beware, driver two jolts and swears—
Tough Luck!

Always keep the reason to have more work next season
Why fix the problem right, keeps us all up at night
Where it stops nobody knows...

Pamela Flanigan

Pamela Flanigan has been a member of the Shelby Writers' Group since 2008 and became the administrator in 2011. For some reason she didn't write much, despite wanting to. She just never tried hard enough. This time, Flanigan did and loved it! She's looking forward to doing more. "Thanks to Sterling Script and a friend who gave me a push."

The Fuss About Guss

Pamela Flanigan

"A Day in the Life" by the Beatles played in my car outside of the bagel store. I didn't wish to leave the warmth for the bitter cold before listening to the most famous final chord in the history of rock and roll. Living with depression and a neurological disease, hereditary spastic paraplegia, has caused me to stop and enjoy the little things, such as a forty second chord in E major. Music is medicine for me. It doesn't help my legs, but it lifts my spirits.

The handicap parking was close to the building, but the walk was long with a cane and cold stiff legs. Wary of tripping on the slightest rise, I walked cautiously, scuffing the cement and sending chunks of salt in all directions. Inside, warm air and the sweet scent of bread and coffee were comforting. Friendly voices filled the store. Despite the comfort, I couldn't linger. There were places to go, things to do, and time flies while moving in slow motion through the day. Getting the bagels was my first stop before the gym.

I left the store with my bag of aromatic baked goods in one hand and my cane in the other.

Outside, I heard something jingle. In my mind, I saw my dad. He carried his keys and loose change in the pockets of his trousers and was often heard before he was seen. A fluffy little floppy eared dog looked up at me. He whined and turned toward the parking lot. He was looking for someone and hopefully someone was looking for him.

In any case, with the cold breeze, we both needed to be someplace warm. His leash was attached to his collar, and it made that familiar jingling sound when he moved. It laid alongside him. A few feet from the door and close to the brick wall was a good place for me to stand because of my difficulty with balance. When I stepped toward him he whined and moved back. I set the bagels down and spoke to him in a soft voice. He looked down and took another step back. Obviously, he was unsure of me. So was I. It would be easy to make a wrong move and go down. We were both unsure of what would happen.

Often, despite the consequences, I just do it. I've had bruises, scrapes, sore muscles, aches and pains because I fall. No humiliation, just frustration. I tumble most often at the gym and try to practice the art of landing. It's been interesting and is definitely a work in progress.

In order to help the dog, I had to find a way to get close to him. I grabbed a bagel, ripped it in half, and left the remaining piece in the bag. I bent over, holding it out in front of me while speaking to him.

He stared at my hand and reached out with his nose to get a whiff.

Slowly, I knelt.

He stepped closer, and as his big dark eyes looked over a frosty mustache, he considered the situation and then grabbed the bite. While he ate, I turned and sat cross-legged so my knees weren't pressing on the cold, hard cement. The dog came even closer and took more. He seemed calm chewing the bagel. I was able to secure his leash. I saw a tag on his collar and hoped for a closer look.

"Hey, let's go and get warm." He gave me a look that said yes. Now, I had to stand, and getting to my feet was difficult, especially in the cold. As I moved, he protested and tried to leave. I spoke softly while wrapping the leash around my wrist. Returning to my hands and knees, I pushed back on my toes and very slowly brought myself to a standing position while bracing against the wall for stability. SUCCESS! Standing by the wall, I picked up my cane and used the leash to bring the dog toward me. Holding onto the bagel bag and the dog while relying on my cane was difficult, but we were close to my car. Slowly but surely, we got there. It was unlocked, so I placed my stuff in the back and opened the driver's door to let my little friend inside. He was reluctant, but was coaxed in with the toe of my shoe. Once inside, he walked to the passenger seat and sat down.

I started the car. The dog seemed calm, looking at me and then back out at the stores. He had to be frightened, but he appeared relaxed. I decided it was a good time to look at the tag. It was small and simply said Guss.

"Guss?" His big dark eyes looked into mine. "Ah, crap. This isn't much help." Using his eyebrows, he asked me to explain myself. "Oh, don't worry, let's just warm up." I pet him, hoping he would relax as we listened to the end of "Eleanor Rigby."

The next song was "Help." It's difficult for me not to sing when I know all the words. So, I sang. "I need somebody. Help, not just anybody. Help, I need someone. Help." Looking outside Guss barked. I stopped singing, but he turned to me and whined. While facing me, his eyebrows spoke, so I continued to sing. I believed we had an understanding. The song and my singing continued along with the occasional accompaniment from Guss. We were having fun.

As the song ended, I noticed white patches of salt on the dark gray cloth of the seat. I didn't want to handle him to see his paws and possibly make him more anxious. So, I took the message from Mother Mary and "Let It Be."

I started singing along to "Here Comes the Sun" as a car

pulled into the lot and parked in the center. Something was familiar to Guss. He stood on the armrest, his ears perked up, and his tail wagged.

A man wearing a tan coat and hat stepped out, looked around, raised his hands to his face, and yelled, "Guss!"

At the same time, Guss barked and howled.

I left the car running, and we got out in no time. The man looked my way, and I intended to yell back, but Guss took care of that. Holding on tight, I let the excited dog lead the way. The owner broke into a short run to reach us. He bent over to pet Guss and expressed how grateful he was to see him. He thanked me while breathing hard. I grabbed a small metal chair that sat near the building and pulled it close. The man sat down and Guss jumped in his lap, his tail wagging as he wiggled, licked, and rubbed up against his beloved friend.

The excitement was contagious. I smiled from ear to ear.

"Okay, okay, Guss. I got ya. We're okay now." The man said to his furry friend as Guss jumped down.

I could hear the emotion in his voice. I surmised they lived alone and the drive to find his dog had been an emotional journey.

Embarrassed, the man stood and straightened his coat. "Thank you so much! Thank you so, so much. I just don't know what happened. When I pulled into the neighborhood, I realized he wasn't there. I always put him in the back. How could I forget him? I don't remember what I did. I feel like a fool." The man's eyes began to well up.

I touched his arm. "Hey, he moves quickly. Something may have caught his eye, and he was gone before you shut the door."

"Well, I can't tell you how much I appreciate what you did. Guss is all I have now." He cleared his throat.

"I don't live alone, but sometimes I think about the unconditional love of a dog. However, you need a good pair of legs to handle one. So, I enjoy other people's dogs."

"Can I ask what happened?" he asked, nodding at my cane.

"It's neurological. I have stiff and weak legs."

"Sorry about that. How did you manage to get Guss in your car?"

"Well, I think this weather helped."

"Yeah, it's cold. Thanks again. I was so worried about him."

"Just so you know, Guss has enjoyed some bagel. He even sang a Beatles song with me."

"The Beatles? Well, Guss, I'm sure that was fun."

"He joined in as I sang 'Help.' I thought it was an appropriate song."

"Yes, it was, and you like to sing, don't you, boy?" He smiled, looking down at Guss. "You were in good hands. Well, let's go home and warm up." He started to turn toward his car then hesitated. "I suppose I'm the fool on the hill with my head in a cloud."

"Actually, he wasn't a fool," I replied. "He saw the sun going down, and the eyes in his head saw the world spinning round. And you're okay, sir. Just double check for Guss when you get in the car."

He smiled, waved goodbye, and turned to walk away, but Guss paused and looked at me as if to say thanks.

I returned to my warm car and music. Smiling, I thought there could be a song about my morning and the fuss about Guss.

Nicole e. Castle

As a writer of weird fiction and poetry, Nicole e. Castle is drawn to what lurks in the shadows. Her publication credits include *Sterling Script: A Local Author Collection, Pink Panther Magazine, Erie Tales, Between the Lines,* and *Recurring Nightmares.*

She is a member of the Great Lakes Association of Horror Writers and editor of their literary horror magazine, *Ghostlight: The Magazine of Terror.*

Castle also teaches English composition and hosts a monthly literary reading series at Macomb Community College's South Campus. Contact her at: weirdnicolewrites@yahoo.com or castlen@macomb.edu.

Watching and Waiting

Nicole e. Castle

I stand outside your door, listening
to the house, its breath on my neck.
I listen for you and try to open the door,
slowly, knowing the doorknob sticks.
Like the old man in Poe's heartless tale,
will your eye fall upon me, and
wonder what the hell I'm doing there?
I can't tell you.
I can't tell you that I'm standing there
to make sure you're still breathing.
I lightly touch your toe, always outside the sheets.
Is your stomach rising? I sweat. Pulse quickens.
I caress your foot. Is it cold?
You turn over, a brief slurp and then silence.
I back out of the bedroom, slumping in the hallway.
I can't walk. I can only listen to my own breath,
shallow but alive.
Each night I stand outside your door, willing
your breath to mingle with the night air, and
slip under the door, touch my face,
as your hands did when I was a child.
Daughter, it whispers, *don't be scared.*
But I am scared. I will continue to wait
outside your door.
Keeping watch.

Afternoon in Jefferstown

Nicole e. Castle

Your mother waits for you.
To bring cabbage
and beans.
To sit with her, watching
fireflies out
the back-porch screen.
To help her into bed, brushing
wispy hair to the
side, setting a kiss
upon her cheek.
Your mother waits for you.
To come by the next day
or maybe the next
or the next.
But you've been waylaid,
outside the grocery.
Cabbage and beans
sit in the passenger seat, waiting
to be cooked and eaten.

A.J. Douglas

A.J. Douglas is a lover of all things fantasy and comedy, especially when they're combined. Her stories are a unique blend of high fantasy elements in a modern-esque world.

She began writing at a young age, publishing fanfiction in high school, and wrote her first novel in her teens. Douglas is a member of the Sterling Heights Creative Writers Workshop and several online writing groups.

She resides in Oakland County with her husband and two sons. Douglas plans to debut her first novel in 2020.

Don't Put All Your Dragon Eggs In One Basket

A.J. Douglas

"Dragon eggs! Get your dragon eggs here!" Delinda shouted over the din of humans and supernatural beings. The Saturday crowd at the outdoor market on the corner of Caldron and Brimstone was always the best day for sales. Today, however, a trio of witches selling love potions for Venus Day were drawing away business. With her father still in recovery from a nasty hydra bite, it was up to her to get the eggs sold.

Voice hoarse, she sunk down in a folding chair next to her boyfriend. After a swig of water, she looked over to him. "What if I try a B.O.G.O?"

Tamil glanced up from his phone. "Lind, what's anyone gonna do with two dragons?"

"Look, I just need to move these stupid eggs before they hatch. My mystery grab bag idea didn't go over well yesterday."

"What's the big deal about that again?"

"Baby dragons imprint on the first living thing they see. Once they accept someone as their master, it's hard to get them to transition to a new one. That's why people prefer to hatch their own."

"Oh, right." He turned back to his phone.

Delinda nudged his foot with hers. "Hey, you're supposed to help me. Quit playing with your phone!"

"You know I have a livestream of Cubicle Qwest that I need to get ready for."

She leaned over to peek at his screen. "Looks more like you're messing around on Faebook and Quiller."

"It's called promoting. Can't gain a following if nobody knows about it."

"I don't know why anyone would want to watch a stream about some boring magic-less world where the only things you slay are papers from your inbox."

"Hey, it's getting really exciting in the cubes! I'm only a few tasks short of my next promotion. Soon my guy will be in upper management. Then it's onto the boss level."

"Whatever," she grumbled. In the real world, office gnomes did the paperwork. Those types of all-human fantasy games with no magic didn't make any sense. But Tamil loved them. Delinda stood and tousled her red curls with her fingers. She hoped her hair wasn't frizzy from the humidity. "Dragon eggs!" she resumed her calling.

Two faeries, arms laden with bags from the high-end clothing store Willow & Birch, floated down the sidewalk. Gold flecks shimmered from their opalescent wings in a cascade that disappeared as it reached the ground.

"Oh, what's this?" One of them stopped, hovering in front of Delinda's table. She lifted her oversize sunglasses from her face.

The second fae popped her gum. "Looks like dragon eggs."

"Oh! I've always wanted a dragon!"

"Well, you're in luck!" Delinda smiled. "They're buy one, get one half-off during the next hour. Better hurry before they're all gone!"

The fae with the sunglasses gasped and grabbed her friend's arm. "We could each get one and raise them together!"

"Right," the second fae said. "Dragons will go over real well back at The Hollow. C'mon." She fluttered past dragging her pouting friend along with her.

Delinda frowned as she watched them go. "Aw, I thought I had them. Faeries love a good bargain."

"Did I hear ya mention a sale?" A wizened old man stepped out from the crowd.

"Yes, sir! My dragon eggs are buy one, get one half-off. Limited time offer! Quality guaranteed. My family is the best in the business."

"How many ya got?"

"I have ten left. Three Elurran Blue Scales, three Solian Sun Flares, two Shamalese Sabre-fangs, and two Raylessian Ridgebacks."

He hummed as he stroked his long, snarled beard. "I'll take 'em all."

Delinda stepped back, blinking several times. "I'm sorry, you said you'd like all of them?"

"That you did, my dear. Hold on, I've got one of them magical expanding bags around here somewhere..." He began to dig around in the pockets of his dark blue cloak. "Ah, here." He removed a small pouch and unfolded it into a khaki canvas tote bag.

"Sir, they're 50 silver a piece at full price."

"Yup, read it on your sign."

"What are you going to do with ten dragon eggs?"

"I've got lots of grandkids. They'll love them!"

She couldn't pass on the chance to unload all of the eggs and be done with this sweltering summer heat. He handed her the money and one by one, each football sized egg disappeared into his tote.

"Remember, you're going to want to keep them in a warm place until they hatch anywhere from three to seven days from now," she said.

He hoisted the bag on his shoulder as if it weighed nothing and left.

Tamil peeled his eyes away from his phone. "He really took them all? Does that mean we're done?"

"Sure does!"

"Isn't your pop gonna be mad that you sold half those eggs at half price?" he asked as they began to pack up.

"Oh, please." Delinda pressed a button on the table. It folded in on itself until it was the size of a briefcase. "He's so hopped up on restorative elixir that he still thinks he has three heads. When I left this morning, he and mom were arguing because each head wanted something different for breakfast."

~ ~ ~

"Alright, everyone, thanks for following along on my journey to the top of Corp-topia!" Tamil's voice announced through the speakers of Delinda's laptop. "Don't forget join me tomorrow, same time, same place, as I prepare to teach the boss a thing or two about synergy!"

Delinda reached over, careful not to smudge her wet nail polish, and pressed her laptop closed. She'd spent the entire livestream on those nails, and wasn't about to let anything ruin them.

Her father was on the mend. He no longer thought he had two extra heads, and the scale-like hives were almost gone. Maybe next time he looked for a new fishing spot, he'll pay attention to what locals tell him lurks beneath the water.

Her mother called her name from outside her bedroom.

"Come in!" she answered, as she lined up a pic of her finished nails for Witch-trest.

Her mother opened the door. She folded her arms, leering at her. "When you sold those eggs a few days ago... Did you sell them all to the same man?"

"Yeah, why?"

Her glare turned incredulous. "Why would you do that?"

"'Cause he wanted to buy them all." Wasn't that obvious?

"Well, he just called. The eggs hatched, and all ten baby dragons have escaped. If they cause trouble, that's our family business's reputation on the line! You need to go and fix this!"

"What? Why do I have to go do it? I have plans tonight!"

"Well, your plans can wait," her mom enunciated, hands on her hips. "You should've known better! And it's your responsibility to fix your mistake. I don't care what you do, or how long it takes. You're not going anywhere until every last baby is accounted for!" Her mom turned and stormed down the hall.

Delinda groaned and flopped back on her bed. Blowing her hair from her face, she reached for her phone and called her boyfriend.

"Hey there, Good Lookin'!" he answered. "Did you get a load of that double-overtime bonus I scored?"

"Tam, we've got a problem. Remember those dragon eggs I sold to that old man? They hatched."

"Isn't that what they're supposed to do?"

"Well, yeah… Anyway, they all escaped, and mom is making me go catch them. Can you help?"

Tamil hesitated. "Babe, I have my post stream A.M.A on Quiller in a few minutes!"

"What, for all twelve of your followers? I really need your help!"

"Fine. But you owe me."

"You're the best! Meet at my place in twenty."

~ ~ ~

Delinda sighed, drumming her hands on the wheel as she drove to the old man's house.

Tamil pocketed his phone. "Calm down, Lind. How much trouble can baby dragons possibly get into?"

She raised her eyebrow. "You don't know much about dragons, do you?"

He shook his head.

"I hope you're ready for a few scratches and maybe a burn or two. Baby dragons are feisty, and since they won't regard us as their masters, they aren't going to be easy to catch." Delinda pulled up in front of the man's home and shut off her car. "I'll go and talk to him, you get the supplies out of the trunk."

After Delinda knocked on his door, the old man answered. "Ah, you're the young lady who sold me my dragons." Half of his beard was scorched and his hands and arms were covered in bandages. From what she could see of his living room, it looked like it had been ransacked by a hoard of baby dragons.

Delinda scuffed her foot across the porch. "Sorry if they caused you any trouble."

"Oh, they certainly did. Turns out the kid's parents weren't too keen on the idea of pet dragons. I tried to hold on to 'em until I could find new homes. But on top of wreckin' the place, they saw a neighbor's cat outside the window. A horned one managed to knock out the screen and all ten of 'em were gone quick as that." He snapped his fingers.

"Don't worry, we'll find every single one," she promised.

When Delinda got back at her car, Tamil held up the large cardboard box they'd brought along. "Are you sure this going to work for creatures that breathe fire?"

"It has a charm that resists it," she answered as she pulled on a pair of hide gloves.

They began in the backyard. "How will we know where to find them?" Tamil asked as he tagged a selfie of him dragon hunting on Quiller.

"First, check under bushes and in trees, or anywhere else that looks like it could be a hiding place. Elurran Blue Scale babies are shy, so they are most likely to hide. After that, follow the chaos."

Behind the man's house, something in a bush growled at them. Since wood nymphs don't inhabit this area, it had to be one of the babies.

Delinda crawled under the bush, parting its bristled boughs. A puff of fire blew towards her face. It missed, but the brush around her smoldered. A tiny dragon with light blue scales that shimmered with hues of silver coiled back, ready to strike again.

She offered the baby a *Dragon De-lite* dragon treat. Once distracted, she swiped the net down and scooped the baby up.

As Delinda tried to back out, her hair became snagged in the bush. She passed the net with the thrashing baby dragon to Tamil, then worked to untangle herself.

Once she was free, her flawless curls now a matted mess, Tamil held the box while she set the dragon inside. Delinda then dropped in a few extra treats before they closed it up.

"Whew!" She wiped her brow. "That went pretty well. Maybe it's a sign that this won't be so bad."

They continued their search of neighboring yards for more dragons. But there weren't any signs of them. "Maybe they all ran off—" she began to say when Tamil stopped her.

He pointed to a grey dragon curled up on a tree branch, fast asleep. "Found one."

"That's a Raylessian Ridgeback. They love to headbutt with those spines, so try to net it while it's still sleeping," she instructed as they approached the tree.

"Why are you telling me this?" Tamil asked.

She thrust the net into his hands. "Because there is no way I am going up that tree after it."

He offered her his phone. "Here, record it then. My Quiller posts are starting to pick up interest."

Delinda rolled her eyes as she took it. She hit "record" as Tamil walked around the base of the tree, sizing it up.

He looked back at her. "Can you come hold the net until I get up there?"

"No, you wanted me to record, so I'm doing just that."

Tamil grumbled under his breath. With the net in one hand, he jumped, taking hold of the lowest branch. He managed to slide the net on top, balancing it so he could let go to grab the branch with both hands. Using his feet to push off the trunk, he pulled himself into the tree.

The baby Ridgeback roused from its sleep with a wide yawn. It smacked its lips as it lifted its head and faced the nap interrupter.

Delinda hissed, "It's awake! Tam! It's awake." She tried to catch his attention without spooking the dragon.

He must not have heard her. One hand wrapped around the tree, he extended the net towards the dragon.

The reptile tilted its head as the net crept closer.

Stretched as far as he could, feet perched precariously on a narrow tree limb, Tamil lowered his net. The Ridgeback launched from its perch and straight for Tamil's face.

He jerked back to avoid the dragon's spines. As he did, his footing slipped. "Whoa!" he cried out, flailing in vain for something to grab on to. "Ahhh!" Tamil crashed to the dirt and roots below.

Wings outstretched, the baby dragon glided down to soft grass nearby.

"Oh my gosh! Tam, are you okay?" Delinda called out as she rushed over to him.

Tamil groaned and raised his head. He found himself face to face with the Ridgeback. It blew a puff of smoke from its nostrils, head lowered.

Tamil scrambled to his feet as the dragon lunged. "Ah! It's chasing me! It's chasing me!" he screamed, doing a lap around the tree, the Ridgeback charging after him.

"Grab the net! Grab the net!" Delinda shouted.

On his next lap, Tamil scooped up the net and spun around to face his foe. The baby leapt for the safety of the tree. Tamil threw himself into a belly flop, netting the dragon as its feet left the ground.

Irate, the creature squealed its displeasure as Tamil carried the net back to Delinda in exchange for his phone.

"Please tell me you got that awesome catch," he said.

Delinda placed the dragon safely into its confinement with the other and left them a few more treats. "Yeah, I got all of it."

He tapped the screen, his tan face blanched, eyes widened in horror. "You live-streamed it?"

"Didn't you say you were doing this live?"

"No! I'm making live *Quills*! I wanted to record a video to edit later. Oh no, it already has loads of views…"

"Oh, well, at least we have another dragon, so that's two down!" Delinda said with a nervous laugh.

They found another Blue Scale holed up in a dog house nearby. Extracting it cost Delinda a bit of her hair. Tamil spotted a Sabre-fang several houses over, chewing up yard decorations. When they caught that one, it tore a gaping hole in their net. They now had four of the ten babies recovered.

As they turned onto the next street, an angry yell erupted from a nearby yard, followed by several crashes.

Delinda and Tamil exchanged looks, and raced towards the sound.

On the other side of a split-rail fence, a man with feathered blond hair ran across his yard waving the charred remains of a broom. Ahead of him, an orange and yellow Solian Sun Flare dashed by, spitting flames in every direction.

The man stopped when he spotted Delinda and Tamil. "Those dirty scamps!" He flung his finger to a destroyed flower bed. "Look what they've done to my peonies!" His eyes fell on the net in Delinda's hands and narrowed. "Are they yours?" he spat.

"No!" Delinda was a little too quick to answer. "I mean… they belong to someone else. We were sent to catch them."

"Just get them out of my sight!" He threw what was left of

his broom to the ground and marched back inside his house.

"Let's get this over with and get out of here." Delinda entered the man's yard, passing a flower bed full of the shredded remains of pink and white peonies, along with twisted and broken stems.

One still standing, yet flowerless plant shook. Out stepped a maroon Shamalese Sabre-fang with a peony blossom in its tiny maw.

Delinda motioned for Tamil to stay still. With as much stealth as she could muster, she crept towards the Sabre-fang as it moved on to its next victim.

The baby twisted and pulled on a mouthful of stems. It uprooted a plant, unaware of the pursuer closing in.

She swung the net down. The captured dragon snagged the already torn netting on its curved, sharp little fangs. The creature thrashed about, shredding what was left of the material.

"No!" Delinda threw herself into the tangle of destroyed flowers and snatched the dragon before it could wriggle itself free. Her hide gloves protected her hands and wrists from an onslaught of teeth and claws as she carried the dragon to where Tamil waited with the box.

As Tamil pried the lid back, a puff of fire blew in his face, followed by the Ridgeback's attempt to scramble out. With his gloved hand, he pushed the dragon back into the box. After Delinda dropped the still thrashing sabre-fang beside it, Tamil slammed the lid shut.

"Do I have any eyebrows left?" he asked.

Delinda focused on his face. "They're a little singed, but mostly there."

"Mostly? At least I'll have a good story to go with it, I guess."

"Sorry about that," Delinda said. "Ridgebacks can be little jerks—they, do you smell something burning?"

Both turned around. A plume of smoke rose from a

corner of the yard. They dashed over to find the Solian Sun Flare in front of a display of decorative wood nymph carvings. Each one set ablaze, burning down to ash. The Sun Flare watched, seeming to admire its handiwork.

Tamil scooped up the distracted dragon before it could find something else to incinerate. It spit flames as Tamil struggled to get a good grip. "Oh no! You little buggers already cost me my eyebrows. You're not getting my hair next!" He aimed the fiery end up and away—straight at an outdoor umbrella. The entire canvas ignited with a *whoosh*.

"What did you do!" Delinda screamed, hands on her head.

"Ah! What do *we* do?" Tamil shouted back, almost dropping the Sun Flare.

"Don't let it go! Put it with the others. I'll look for a hose!"

Delinda searched along the house, breathing a sigh of relief when she found one around the corner.

After the flames were extinguished, Tamil approached her with the box. The front of his shirt torn to shreds.

"What happened to you?" Her eyes widened.

"The Ridgeback happened," he fumed through gritted teeth.

Delinda cringed. "Well, at least we're more than half-way there." She looked at the destruction around her. "Let's head back to my car for a quick break."

"I look like a mess," Delinda examined herself in her rear-view mirror. Her hair was a frizzed, tangled heap. At least the burned part could be taken care of with a trim. Both of them were smudged with dirt and grime, and Tamil's shirt was a lost cause.

"At least you still have your eyebrows," Tamil grumbled.

As Delinda picked bits of plant matter from the bush out of her hair, two women walking a pet gremlin passed by. Some of their conversation drifted in through her open car window.

"...That's what I heard. They set Willow & Birch on fire. I hope Magical Animal Control can get to them before they cause any more trouble..."

"Oh no!" Delinda gasped. "Tam, we need to go, I think I found some of our missing dragons," she said as she started her car.

"Do you really think we're going to beat Magical Animal Control there if it is our dragons?" Tamil asked as Delinda sped through town.

"No idea, but it's worth a try."

A crowd was gathered around the store front. A police fae kept people back while fire department wizards used magic to extinguish the last of the flames. Plumes of dark smoke wafted through shattered display windows, and with it was the smell of burnt wood and fabric.

"What happened here?" Delinda asked as they approached the crowd of gawkers.

"A pair of baby dragons got inside," a girl answered her. "When someone tried to catch them, they started spitting fire everywhere. The entire store went up in flames."

Delinda and Tamil cringed as they exchanged glances. "What happened to the dragons?" Delinda asked, not sure if she wanted the answer.

"Magical Animal Control took them away a little bit ago."

Delinda thanked her and they left. "My parents are going to be furious! Like, grounded for the rest of high school, furious," she said on the walk back to her car.

"At least we know where two of the dragons are though, and for now they are safe," Tamil tried to offer some form of reassurance.

"I know, but ugh, what a mess this turned into. I should have known better than to sell that man all ten eggs."

Once back in her car, Tamil checked his phone. "This thing has been blowing up like crazy with notifications." He tapped at the screen. "Well, the day has officially gotten

worse. Not only has that video gone viral, I'm now a meme."
He turned his phone towards her and scrolled through a
comments section full of screen grabs and gifs from the video
with funny captions added to them.

"Well, you always did want to be an internet sensation,
and look at your follower count now." She tried her best to
sound supportive.

He raised a burnt eyebrow at her. "Yeah, in gaming. But
followers are good. I just hope they don't think I chase
dragons and fall out of trees all the time."

As they drove, discussing their next course of action, a
black cat darted in front of her car. Delinda slammed on the
breaks in time, but the cat didn't stop. It scampered across
the road, as other cars screeched to a halt. Another black cat
followed behind it. This one eliciting honks from impatient
drivers. Then two more.

"Uh, Lind…" Tamil tapped her on the shoulder.

"What?" She looked over. Her eyes widened at the sight of
a hoard of black cats barreling out into the road. Behind them
was the baby Raylessian Ridgeback. Once the cats ran past,
she pulled the car over into the next empty spot and jumped
out with the engine still running.

"Wait, come back!" she cried out after it, waving the bag
of *Dragon De-lites* in vain. The Ridgeback was clearly having
too much fun.

Cats scurried in all different directions, startling people
and causing cars to slam on their brakes. Horns blared.
Delinda lost sight of the ridgeback in the chaos. She heard
Tamil call her name, and turned to see him running to catch
up with her. "I lost track of it!" she shouted to him. "We
need to find it, quick!"

People screamed and scattered as cats ran over their feet
and between their legs. Signs and shop displays were toppled
over by terrified cats. One jumped onto a window sill,
knocking over a flower pot in the process.

Delinda caught sight of the Ridgeback as it chased some cats around the corner. She followed after the dragon, determined not to lose sight of it.

Tamil caught up as they were closing in.

The dragon paused for the slightest instant. The first signs of tiring.

Delinda took the opportunity and lunged, landing on pavement as she snatched the dragon around its hind legs.

The dragon turned, ready to head-butt her. Tamil picked it up before it could attack. It fought his grip, until Delinda offered it a treat. The dragon didn't hesitate to gobble it up.

"Even baby dragons get tired and hungry, eventually." Delinda patted it on the head as she offered it another treat.

She and Tamil returned to her car. They could feel the angry stares of passersby in the aftermath of the chaos. A few people even yelled choice words at them.

"At least my car is still here," Delinda said, relieved at the sight of it parked where she left it.

"Oh, right." Tamil reached into his back pocket. "I grabbed your keys for you."

"Thanks. You really are the best."

Tamil shrugged. "Isn't that what boyfriends are for?"

The box of dragons in her back seat was suspiciously calm. Delinda peeked under the lid, relieved to find the babies curled up, fast asleep. She placed the tired Ridgeback in with the others.

"Now we need to figure out where the last one is," she said as they climbed into the front seat.

"Do we even know what's left?" Tamil asked.

Delinda thought it over. "I think it's a Blue Scale... I'm willing to bet the captured two were Sun Flares, on account of the fires. If it is a Blue Scale, it could be hiding anywhere."

"We could always go back and re-trace our earlier steps. The other two we found were close to that old man's house."

"Good idea as any." Delinda put the car in gear.

When they returned to the old man's house, he stepped outside, the last Blue Scale curled up in his arms. "Turns out not all of them escaped," he greeted them. "Found this little one hiding under my couch. I'd like to keep 'im, except I don't have room for a dragon here." He looked the two of them up and down. "Sure looks like you two have had it rough."

Delinda and Tamil looked at each other. They couldn't help but laugh as Delinda accepted the dragon from the old man.

~ ~ ~

"Hey, Lind," Tamil answered his phone. "What's up?"

"Just thought I'd update you on the dragon situation," Delinda held her phone against her ear with her shoulder as she leaned back in a chair at her kitchen table. "My parents were able to get the two Sun Flares back from animal control, and most of Willow & Birch was able to be fixed with magic, but I'm still in serious trouble."

"That's good, that they got the dragons out I mean. What is going to happen to them?"

"My mom found a dragon riding academy that will take them. Since they aren't fully imprinted, they should work out. How've you been?"

Tamil sighed. "Oh, you know, enjoying my new status as the viral internet sensation of the week. But my finale of Cubicle Qwest went well."

"Wish I could have seen it, but I've had my hands full tending to all those baby dragons until they go to their new home. I swear if I get head-butted by a Ridgeback one more time…I might just lose it."

Tamil laughed. "I think I'll be happy if I never have to help out with your family's dragon business ever again."

"Yeah, me too!" Delinda laughed with him.

Zan Giese

Zan Giese decided she would be a writer at the age of five and hasn't stopped writing since. A graduate of Oakland University, she dabbles in flash fiction, short stories, and novels. When she's not writing, she spoils her dog, Spike.

The Psychic's Son

Zan Giese

My brother was in love with the psychic's son. A boy with no talent for discerning the lines of palms or the dregs of your tea. He saw no deeper meaning in your dreams, and the charts of the stars had no correlation to your birth.

When he was younger, he pretended to read palms. But he only foretold death. Or he did until a teacher overheard and gave him detention for two weeks.

And then he got older. He handled the clients, their information, the lighting of incense, and finding the appropriate level of darkness. And this is the boy that my brother fell in love with. The boy who smelled like sandalwood and sage. The boy with dark hair and gray eyes like wet ashes. And it was a gross love: hand holding, eye gazing, sweet talking and promises of forever no matter who was around. The kind of love you don't really think exists, because people don't act like that. There's just no way. It's supposed to be hard, and vulnerability must be earned and private.

The psychic took one look at my brother and said, "Do not get comfortable."

She left a tray of tea with them and returned downstairs. She refused to call my brother by his name. Always Jeremy, Samuel, Ron. A different name every day. Sometimes a different name each time she talked to him.

It was a story that ended with twisted metal and shattered glass on the bridge just outside of town. With the engine ticking and the headlights still blaring out into the darkness of the rainy night.

And the news traveled through the telephone wires, static whispers, moving like hair down the drain. I wasn't home when my parents heard.

I saw the psychic's son with his dark hair and his pebbly eyes at the grocery store a year later. I saw him under the timed fluorescent lighting. Wavering, humming tubes of light. He had one of those black baskets and a bottle of whiskey. He had stubble and careless hair.

"Did your mother know?" I asked. "Did your mother predict his death? Did she tell you?"

He had not seen me before that moment, but his body jerked to the sound of my voice. To the nature of my questions. The flinch rolled through him, and I saw his chest catch a breath and hold onto it like a wounded bird. His fingers tightened around the neck of the whiskey bottle.

He did not come any closer. We stared at each other across the space between the potato chips and the frozen foods over the steady hum of the freezers.

"Jesus Christ," he said. "What do you want me to say?"

"The truth," I said.

"Yes," he said.

The word barreled through me, and I watched him walk away with his basket and his alcohol. I watched the psychic's son head down the water aisle as a long breath left me. I stood still long enough to catch the attention of a passing employee.

"Can I help you find something?" he asked.

"No," I said. I set down the bag of chips that had been in my hand, and I left the store. Heading out into the cool air of the evening.

The Language of Shadows

Zan Giese

"It's biblical," Dmitri said, blood running down his wrist and dripping scarlet against the tile floor. "Brother trying to kill brother."

"It's stupid," Conri said. He held medical gauze in hand and vexation in heart.

Dmitri grinned before lighting a cigarette. He took a slow drag from it, the end burning a brilliant orange. The blood droplets multiplied on the floor like a bad painting.

Conri leaned over and cracked open the bathroom window. He set down the gauze and rolled up Dmitri's sleeve, inspecting the wound. "What did he get you with?"

"Something sharp. I got him back. He's still alive though."

"He's your brother."

Dmitri wasn't sure if it was a question or a statement. It acted like both; it acted like neither. He smoked his cigarette and looked up toward the smooth ceiling above him.

Conri snatched a pale hand towel off the ring by the sink. He ran warm water over it, soaking the fabric, and then he washed out the wound. "You'll need stitches."

"Can you do it? I don't like hospitals," Dmitri said, gritting his teeth. His eyes were a brighter silver than their normal washed out gray.

Conri frowned. He set his hand over the wound. There

was a brilliant white light, and the wound closed. It left them both winded. Conri went back to wiping up the blood off his arm with the rag that used to be a towel.

Dmitri had sucked in a breath of air between his teeth. He considered his arm, lifting and rotating it. "That hurt," he said. There was a beat as he examined the skin where once there had been a laceration. "It's healed."

Conri took the rag to the sink and rinsed the blood out of it. A coppery smell hung thick in the air, and he wrinkled his nose as he soaked the rag with cold water before wringing it out until the water ran red and then pink and then a lighter pink. Never quite clear.

Dmitri finished his cigarette. The smoke trailed toward the ceiling. He disposed of the rest of it and looked toward Conri standing in front of the sink, hands holding the saturated cloth. "You're mad."

Tension straightened Conri's shoulders. He squeezed the water from the rag, twisting it between his palms. Dmitri watched the pink water swirl around the sink before rolling down the drain.

"Conri, talk to me," he said.

"It's two in the morning. You showed up and asked me to stitch you up like it's nothing," Conri said finally, the rag bunched up between his fingers.

Dmitri rose from his seat and came over to the other man, setting his hand on his hip. He felt the tension underneath his fingers, and he studied his reflection in the mirror. "I just asked in case you could. I didn't want to wait," he said.

"You just said you didn't like hospitals," Conri said. He set the rag on the side of the sink. He glanced at Dmitri, golden eyes ablaze.

"Both can be true."

"Damnit, Dmitri. I'm your boyfriend, not someone you need to lie to," he snapped.

Dmitri lifted his hand from Conri's hip and reached for

his hand. The tension flared into the room. He saw the crease form between Conri's eyebrows.

Conri's frown deepened. "What's your next lie?"

"I'm not lying to you," Dmitri said.

"I'm going downstairs to make some tea. You are welcome to join me if you like, but I don't want to continue this discussion right now," Conri said. He left the small bathroom where they had been crowded together. It had not necessarily been a space designed for two men to occupy at the same time. Dmitri heard his footsteps move down the hall and then descend the stairs. He thought quietly of Orpheus.

And then of his brother. His sudden appearance outside the diner. His eyes small, dark, and glittering like beetles. His hair flaxen and boring, an opposite to Dmitri in every way. His brother looked every aspect their father.

Dmitri needed to get rid of him. Whatever that meant. Whatever that took.

The people of Willowvale said Dmitri had no soul, that he was the devil himself. Dmitri only smiled at those rumors: the devil was his father. And if he were any kind of devil, Dmitri had learned it from him.

Roots

Zan Giese

Ava tangled her fingers into the green and yellow blades of grass and thought of roots. She imagined them springing up and wrapping around her wrists, small leaves like precious stones, all of it holding her into place. She closed her eyes. She had read somewhere that trees spoke Latin and lamented her choice to study German. Releasing the grass, she fell back onto her butt and sat underneath the biggest tree she had been able to find.

In the distance, she saw two women ducking through the trails and following the creek as it carved through the land. They were heading toward a small wooden bridge she always called Hemingway Bridge for no other fact than it was a very simple construct. Ava liked to sit on it and watch the creek carry away twigs and other bits and bobs that had fallen into the water. The girls were quickly out of view and just as quickly out of her thoughts.

Spring had charged in with the ferocity of July. Ava did not look forward to what the actual summer was going to be like. Even in the shade of the tree, sweat gathered and slid along her skin. Ava felt it on her lower back and behind her knees. She was half-tempted to throw herself into the creek, but it was a long walk back to campus and an even longer walk back to her apartment. The chafing from wet jean shorts would not be worth it.

For a long time, she just sat under the shadow of the tree. She tilted her head up, peering through the budding branches at the blue sky. Ava closed her eyes, wanting to bottle up the quiet and the warmth for the bad days. For the gray days when the effort to get out of bed was overwhelming. For the days when she felt like a pond instead of the sea.

The walk back to campus was quiet when she finally pushed herself up. It was late enough that most of the student population had dispersed, trickling out of the parking lot like sand from an hourglass. And it was still just as hot, maybe even hotter. Perhaps there would be no relief from the heat. She forced her legs to carry her forward through campus and back to the rows of apartment buildings. The end of the semester was quickly approaching, and Ava had been packing her things, preparing for her inevitable return to a small town with big city aspirations. To a town where her mother would introduce her always as Liam's sister.

To which, some people, usually men, would say, "Oh, Liam, I like him," in very much a tone that said I do not, however, care for this girl you're introducing me to.

Ava did not begrudge them this. At least, not too much. She was a creature in-between, and her brother was someone with a ready ear, always eager to give anyone a chance. It was as easy for him as breathing. Ava wore her apprehension for other people like spikes.

She showered and changed into clothes that she had not spent the afternoon sweating in. She packed clothes that she wouldn't need in the upcoming days, her books, and her knick knacks which made this place feel more like the home that was over two hundred miles away. It was a lot to carry over the distance for two semesters worth of staying, but it helped when everyone else in her life was so far away.

Maybe this summer would be better. Maybe she could be gentle like dear Liam. It was about as likely as her mother introducing her as only Ava. Her existence not defined by her brother's. Perhaps she could be the sea during the whole season, not reducing herself to puddles or ponds.

Ava closed a box and then taped its flaps. She thought of the tree she had sat under earlier. She thought of the grass and the roots. The tangles in her stomach, the thoughts of home, all relaxed, and she took a breath. And then another. Ava stood in her room, satisfied she had managed to capture that feeling from underneath the tree.

Marie Thrynn

Marie Thrynn is a domestic poet who dwells in Michigan and the land of anxiety. She grew up in the Sterling Heights library and prefers the company of books.

Spilled

Artist: Marie Thrynn

One more thing

Marie Thrynn

Hot water on for tea.
      But first,

                Collect the spices spilled on the stove,
                    while I
                Fill the pitcher to filter the water,
                    while I
                Take out a pot (there's no kettle).

Boil the water,
    while I
Clear the onion skins staining the counter,
    while I
Rummage for a mug for the tea.

                        One more thing—
                    when was the last time I...

Ran some vinegar through the coffee maker
(so the kitchen smells like acid)
while I
Gather the lost grit of grounds
while I
Smear away the missed brown drips.

Pour the bubbling water for the tea,
while I
Wipe the drips and click off the heat and turn into my mother
while I
Finish one more thing.

Steep the tea,
while I
Sweep the floor
(because the crumbs are bleeding through my socks)
while I
Drop the dustpan and have to scoop it up again.

Taste the cold tea,
while I
Dump the vinegar-water coffee pot,
while I
Bring the water to a boil again.

Rena Davis

Rena Davis is a retired Army Sergeant currently residing in Sterling Heights, Michigan. She is married to Jason Davis, and they have five kids. Though she is busy taking care of her family, writing has become her passion.

This is her second contribution to *Sterling Script: A Local Author Collection.* Her first submission, "Army Strong," was her debut into the writing world. She is currently running a website entitled Book Haven which does book reviews and articles on writing. She has also created a publishing company, Conteur Publishing, which she is trying to grow as a small indie publisher.

Her current project is her *Legion* novella series. An excerpt from book one of that series is included in this collection of stories. Book one will be released in August 2019.

Murder In The Heights

Rena Davis

"Come on, Arway. The night is young, and we still have a lot of partying to do," said Patience as the girls were leaving Club Rave.

"Yeah, come with us," echoed June.

"Guys, I'm beat. I'm gonna head home. I'll see you two tomorrow." Arway gave the girls hugs and kisses.

Strolling the four blocks back to her Downtown Heights apartment, Arway couldn't help but feel like she was being followed. Paranoid, she picked up the pace. She unlocked the door to her apartment building just as another tenant was approaching with his key.

"Fun night?" the young man asked.

"Oh, yeah. It's my birthday so I went out with my girls." She pushed her curly dark brown hair behind her ear. "You?"

"Not so fun. Work event."

The two continued their small talk as they rode up in the elevator.

"Well, goodnight," Arway said as she exited on her floor.

"Goodnight." The young man said as the elevator door closed.

~ ~ ~

Victoria woke to her cell phone blaring. Instinctively she reached out, eyes closed and picked up her phone.

"Hello."

"Wake up, Victoria. We got a crime scene."

"What? What time is it?"

"It's four in the morning. Get up lazy bones. I'll text you the address."

"Ok."

What the hell? Why can't bodies be found at like noon? Victoria stalked to the bathroom. After a couple splashes of water to the face, she was wide awake. She grabbed her coffee, gun, and badge and sprinted out the door.

"Nice of you to join us," Michael said with a playfulness in his voice. He was standing next to the body taking notes.

"Not now, Michael. I'm only on my first cup of coffee." She knelt down by the body. "So what do we have here?"

"Victim's name is Arway Duncan." Michael's green eyes were fixed on his notepad. "Her roommate found her around 3:15 a.m."

"Did you get a statement from her yet?"

"No, you know how I am about crying women."

"Men, I swear." *Humans, I swear.* Victoria walked over to the weeping roommate. There was a beat cop trying his best to console her. "Hi, my name is Victoria. I am one of the detectives assigned to this case. Do you mind if I ask you a few questions?"

"Icantbelieveshe'sdeadwhatamigoingtodo," said the girl, sobbing her eyes out.

"I understand this is a difficult time, but I need you to relax and talk to me." Victoria sat down beside her and placed a healing hand on her back. A gesture that always calmed humans. "Let's start with an easy question. What's your name?" A slight white light radiated from her hand as she sent her magic into the witness. Victoria was always amazed at how humans could never see the magic around them.

"Stacey."

"Good, good. Stacey, can you tell me what happened?"

"I don't know. I came home after a fight with my boyfriend, but when I walked in there she was. Tied to a chair. Dead."

"Did she have any enemies or trouble with anyone that you know of?"

"No. Everyone loved Arway. She was one of those people who would give you the shirt off her back if you needed it, whether she knew you or not."

"Did she have a boyfriend or girlfriend?"

"Um, no." Stacey sniffled and reached for the box of tissues next to the couch.

"Do you know what she did last night or who she might have been with?"

"It was her birthday, so a couple of close friends and I took her club hopping. That's why my boyfriend and I were fighting. He was upset I was out partying, so I left early to have it out with him."

"Can you tell me the other girls' names?" Victoria dropped her hand from Stacey's back. She looked up and saw her partner, Michael, writing in his notepad.

"Patience and June." She blew her nose into the tissue.

"Thank you, that's all for now."

"I should have stayed with her," she said to no one in particular. "Maybe if I had stayed with her, maybe this wouldn't have happened."

"You can't think like that," Victoria said. "I promise you I will do everything I can to get to the bottom of this."

As Victoria started to stand, Stacey grabbed her hand. "Thank you."

~ ~ ~

"Hold on!" yelled a voice behind the door.

Patience opened the door to her studio apartment and was face to face with a detective.

"Hi, are you Patience McRoy?" Victoria asked.

"Yes, what is this about? I'm running late for work."

191

"Do you know an Arway Duncan?"

"Yes."

"May I come in?"

"What is this about?"

"I'm sorry to inform you that she was found murdered this morning in her apartment."

"You can't be serious," Patience said, slowly stepping back while shaking her head.

"I'm sorry, but it's true."

Patience dropped to her knees and the tears poured from her eyes. "I was just with her last night."

"I know that this is a hard time, but I need to ask you a few questions. Can I come in?"

She waved Victoria forward. Victoria knelt down beside her for an embrace. She helped Patience up and walked her over to her couch. "Can you tell me where you were last night?"

"We took Arway out to the clubs for her birthday." She reached for a tissue and blew her nose. "Arway wasn't really the party type but her roommate and I talked her into it. Does her roommate know?"

"Yes, unfortunately she was the one who found the body." Patience's cries rose louder and more hysterical. Victoria grabbed her a water bottle from the kitchen counter. "Here, drink some of this. Can you tell me who all was there?"

Patience took a long swig of the water. "It was me, Stacey, and June, but Stacey left early. She was fighting with her boyfriend. Again."

Victoria's pants were buzzing. "I'm sorry, can you give me a minute?" Victoria stepped away to answer her phone. "Yeah, what's up."

"Hey, I just talked to June." Michael said.

"Anything interesting?"

"No, not really. They went to the club and left the victim around midnight out front of Club Rave."

"Okay, I am here with Patience now."

"I did hear something interesting from the coroner's office. There was a symbol carved on the victim's back."

"What kind of symbol?"

"No one knows. I'm gonna head back to the office and start researching it."

"Ok, I will be there to help as soon as I'm done here." Victoria hung up the phone and turned back to Patience.

"Where were we?" Victoria said, looking at her notes. "Where did you go when you left Arway?"

"June and I headed to another club. We tried talking Arway into going, but she just wanted to go home."

"Do you know anyone that would want to hurt her?"

"No, everyone loved her."

Victoria looked down at her phone. Michael had sent her a text with the picture of the symbol. "Does this symbol mean anything to you?"

Patience stared, eyes locked on the phone. Her eyes went wide but quickly returned to normal. "No, no, it means nothing to me. Um, I have to get myself together and go to work, so if there are no more questions I really need to get a move on."

"Ok, well, thank you for your time." Victoria walked to the door. She handed Patience her business card. "If you think of anything else, give me a call."

And with that Patience closed the door. Victoria walked to her car. She couldn't help but notice that things took a turn to the weird side towards the end. *A human wouldn't have noticed. Bad thing for her, I wasn't human.*

~ ~ ~

Victoria walked into the precinct with her third mug of coffee in hand. The office was bustling with the sounds of perps being walked in and cops participating in water cooler chatter. Placing her coffee on her desk, she plopped in her chair.

"Hey, I thought you were avoiding coming back to the office." Michael said.

"And why would I do that?" She leaned back in her chair and kicked her feet up on her desk. "I love it here."

"Yeah, ok." He rolled his eyes. "I've been trying to figure this symbol out but I am at a loss. Every time I try to search it keeps coming up with some crap about faeries. Ridiculous, right?" He chuckled.

"Yeah." She knew what she had to do. She would have to talk to the King and Queen, aka her parents, in order to get to the meaning of this symbol. She was starting to zone out when she heard the ringing of her partners phone.

Michael fished for his phone in his pocket. "Hello."

"Hey, Mike, I got another one for you," said a male cop on the phone.

"What you got."

"Female. Tortured then killed. She has the same symbol carved on her back as well."

"Really. We'll be there shortly. Bye." Michael hung up his phone and stuck it back into his pocket. "Seems like we have another victim by the same killer. Let's go, partner."

Michael and Victoria arrived at the scene of the second murder. The victims were similar in look and build. The same symbol was carved on her back as well. Victoria knew she couldn't procrastinate any longer. It was time to see the parents. She left Mike to wrap up the crime scene, caught a ride with an "Uni" to her car and headed to Mom and Dad's.

She pulled into the driveway of the gate house. A cute little cottage sat on the front of the property. It's a very modest house by design to discourage any interest in what nestled behind it. After the guards unlocked the iron gate behind the house, she drove the five miles down the path to the main house.

Light Faerie Manor is what you would expect it to look like. A huge mansion full of light, warmth, and lots of windows. Victoria loved growing up here. But now it was a reminder of a world she was trying to run away from. Arranged marriages and royal politics. She didn't want anything to do with that world.

Victoria parked in front of the main door to the house for a fast exit. She marched straight to the throne room where she knew her parents would be holding court.

"Mother. Father." She walked up to them sitting on their diase.

"My daughter," her mother said, walking toward her with open arms. "It's so wonderful to see you, my dear. You have been away for much too long."

"Are you sure about that?" Victoria pulled away from her mother. "The last time I was here, you said I was a disgrace to the family."

"My daughter, I believe we both said things in the heat of the moment. It doesn't mean I love you any less."

"I'm not here about that any way. There were two murders with one common thread, a symbol carved in their back." Victoria handed her mother her phone with the picture pulled up on it. "I was hoping you could tell me what it was, and what does it mean?"

Her mother's eyes went ice cold. There was a rage in those eye's Victoria had never seen before.

"It is a symbol of a faerie house." Her mom sat back down on her throne. "You said there were two murders?"

"Yes. The first victim was Arway Duncan. I don't have a name for the second victim yet."

The Faerie Queen looked at her husband. There were flashes of hurt, concern, and anger across their faces. Whatever this symbol meant, it was not good.

Her father reached for his wife's hand. "I think it's time that we tell her."

"But Tristan," the queen covered her husband's hand with her free hand. "The burden is ours, not hers."

"What are you guys talking about?" Victoria walked up the steps of the diase. "What burden?"

Her father walked to her, took her hand, and they sat down on the steps. "As you know, I grew up in the mortal world with my mother. What you don't know is that my mother hid me among the mortals for most of my childhood. She was afraid that I would be taken from her or worse, killed. She had slept with the king and got pregnant. My mom was not of royal blood. She was a commoner, and it was unheard of for kids of royal blood to be amongst the common folk."

Victoria fidgeted in place. She was thrown aback with the sadness in her father's eyes. "What happened?"

"Well, she went to her friends in the palace, three midwives, for help. Arway, Katerina, and Rebecca, they are sisters. That symbol on your victims is their crest. The dark queen found out about the pregnancy, and, before she could order my mother's death, her friends helped her escape and hide with mortals."

Victoria turned and looked at her king. "Father, are you saying these murders are about you?"

"Maybe. You must be careful, my darling." He stood pulling Victoria up with him.

The queen stood and met her husband and daughter. "Yes, be careful."

"Guys, I'm always careful. Don't worry."

Victoria got as much information as she could from her father about these three sister midwives before she headed back to the station. Now she knew what the symbol meant but how was she going to use that information to apprehend the killer. It's not like she could walk into the police station and say, "Hey guys, it's a faerie killing thing. Don't worry about it."

She couldn't tell Michael she knows what the symbols mean without explaining the history behind it. Maybe the second victim won't be one of the sisters. But that would mean she would be back at square one if that was the case. This was why she hated living in two worlds, but it was also why she had to. There would be no justice for these women otherwise.

"Hey, partner," Michael said as Victoria strolled in to her desk.

"Hey. Do we have a name for the second victim yet?"

Michael flipped through his handy dandy notebook. "Yeah, it is Rebecca Deluth, the first victim's sister according to the M.E."

"So we have two victims, both with that symbol carved into them. Did you find out more about the symbol?" Victoria sat down in her chair facing her partner.

"No, I haven't."

"What if it's some kind of family crest?"

"That's a huge leap, but maybe. It could be possible," Michael said.

"We should go back to the house and take a better look ourselves."

Michael looked confused. "Why? CSI has already been all over that place."

"We need to find the connections between these women, and that symbol. If it is a family crest there should be some remnant of it in their places right?"

"I guess."

"So, come on detective. Let's go detect."

Victoria and Michael headed to Arway's house first in search for more information on her and her family. Of course she knew what she was searching for, even if Michael didn't. She found a picture of three women. It was in a trunk in the back of her closet. Victoria assumed it was Arway and her sisters. She opened the frame and saw that their names were written on the back. Arway, Katerina, and Rebecca. They continued to search to find anything with that symbol on it to no avail. If Arway had a family crest, it was either gone or never here to begin with.

They continued their search at Rebecca's house. She searched her closet and found nothing. As she was searching her night stands, she found a key.

"Find anything?" Michael yelled from the living room.

"Maybe." She yelled back as she walked in to the living room. "I found this key to a storage facility. According to the tag it's Platinum Storage."

"Well, let's go check it out."

Reluctantly, Victoria said, "Okay."

When they reached Platinum Storage, Victoria felt a strangeness she had never felt before. It was power, radiating power it seemed from multiple sources. She followed that sensation to storage unit 258. She was afraid to open it with Michael there. There was no telling what could happen. She inserted the key, braced herself, and turned to unlock the unit. Michael lifted the gate and Victoria's hazel eyes went wide. It was set up like an infirmary for faeries.

Lucky for Victoria, there was the symbol etched on the patient beds inside. As they searched the files, they found a name and number for the third sister, Katerina Duncan. They called it in and requested the address for Katerina.

"Let me do all the talking," Victoria said to Michael.

"Sure thing."

Knock, Knock, Knock. There was no answer so she knocked again. Knock, Knock, Knock.

"Do you hear that?" Victoria whispered to Michael.

"No."

"It sounds like someone crying for help."

"I didn't hear anything."

Victoria heard the muffled cry for help again and busted through the door. This time she wasn't going to wait. As they entered the cries grew louder and they followed it to where Katerina was, tied to a chair and beaten. The assailant was dressed in all black with a black ski mask on. One look at the detectives and he took off. Victoria ran to the victim while Michael went after the assailant.

"Are you okay?" Victoria asked Katerina.

"I am now. If you didn't bust in when you did, I would surely be dead right now."

Victoria started untying Katerina. "Do you know who that was?"

"No." She said.

"What did he want?"

"He wanted to know about a birth, many years ago, in which my sisters and I were the midwives."

"What did you tell him?"

"Nothing. I told him nothing."

"Do you even know who it is this guy is looking for?"

"No." Her eyes said yes.

"I lost him," Michael said as he stumbled in out of breath. He hunched over, hands on his knees, panting. Trying to catch his breath.

"We need to get her to a safe house," Victoria said as she walked toward Michael. She thought he sounded like an asthmatic mid attack.

"Okay." He said between pants. "I'll set it up."

Katerina, with Victoria's help, gathered her things for the safe house. The car was eerily silent the whole trip. Katerina was still in shock from the attack because she definitely did not notice who Victoria actually was, or so Victoria assumed.

They pulled up to a secluded cabin in the woods. Victoria thought to herself that this was a perfect hideout. There was no way Katerina would be found out here. Michael dropped the girls off and went into town for some supplies. Seclusion also meant no food out here, so someone had to get provisions. Thankfully, Michael volunteered. The girls settled into the cabin, starting a fire in the fireplace and claiming sleeping space.

"Are you sure you don't know who they are looking for?" Victoria asked Katerina.

She finally actually looked at Victoria, seeing her eyes. Katerina's eyes went wide. "I think you know, my child."

"Me? How would I know?"

Katerina leaned forward staring into Victoria's eyes. "These humans may think you as one of them, but I know the truth. For it is I who brought your father into this world."

"WHAT?!"

"I suspect you already knew that. I suspect you have been told of how your father was brought into this world. But do you know of the dangers of it?"

"What dangers? Other than my grandmother being common, I don't see what dangers there can be."

"Your father was created out of love, actual love, between the Dark Faerie King and a common dark faerie."

"Okay. I still don't see the danger in that other than a bitter Dark Queen."

"Their union produced your father and with that love came an unbelievable amount of power, for love is the strongest power in the universe. As of right now, they think he is the strongest power in the world. But they are mistaken." Katerina sat back in her lounge chair and stared at the fire.

"Who is then?" Victoria asked leaning forward intently hanging on Katerina's every word.

"Your father was made out of love, unlike the kids he has with the actual Dark Queen, which means he is the strongest of his siblings, yes, but not in the universe. Luckily, they are only concerned with the strongest of the Dark Faeries, which means that they are looking to destroy your father so that the current Dark King will be the most powerful. And we must keep it that way. They must never find out about your father or I fear they may find out..." She trailed off looking back at the fire.

"They may find out about what?" Victoria asked.

"Find out about you."

"ME!? Why would I matter? I am a light faerie who has renounced her family's business."

"What you choose to do with your life has no effect on the power you still possess. You have two parents both made out of love. Powerful as they are separate, their combined powers now grow within you. This is why there has always been arranged marriages, to avoid this type of concentration of power. You, my dear, can rule them all. Dark and Light."

"Hey, girls, I'm back," Michael said strolling in with his arms full of groceries.

Victoria sat frozen in her seat with the weight of the information that was just dumped on her.

"Victoria, are you okay?" Michael asked as he started putting the groceries away.

She snapped out of her inner spiral. "Yeah, I was just zoning out."

"Here," he said as he handed her and Katerina a bottle of water.

"Thanks," the girls said in unison.

Victoria took a swig of her water, and then another. Suddenly she started to feel light headed. Within a minute she was out and so was Katerina. When they awoke, they were both tied to the dining room chairs.

Victoria struggled against the ropes. "What the hell is going on?" She looked around the room to see Michael laying out his "tools." "Michael, what is going on?"

"What's going on is you helped me find the last sister. The last person who knows the Dark King's dirty little secret. Once we dispose of her, there will be no one to contest the Dark Prince's rise to the throne."

"What the hell are you talking about, Michael? Why are you helping them?"

"Sweet, little Katerina, here is my ticket in to a life filled with magic. Once I deliver the information inside her head, they are going to make me a faerie."

"Ha ha ha ha. Are you serious? Do you actually think it works that way? Besides, aren't you the one that said the idea of faeries was ridiculous?"

"Yes, I was, but I didn't really mean it. I have seen them, Victoria. Really seen them. And now, I will be one of them."

"Michael, don't do this."

"Oh, I'm not going to do anything." He looked toward the front door as it flung open. "He is."

Katerina eyes widened with recognition. "Zeke."

"Hello. Katerina." Zeke stalked over to Katerina.

Victoria struggled within her restraints discreetly. She avoided using faerie magic because she didn't want Zeke or even Michael to figure out what and who she was. Zeke pulled out his knife and dragged it ever-so-lightly down Katerina's right cheek. Victoria had finally broken free from her rope shackles. Zeke walked over to the table of tools Michael had laid out.

"Where shall we begin?" Zeke ran his fingers over the tools, settling on a scalpel.

"How about with this?" Victoria swung the chair across the back of Zeke's head. He collapsed on the floor. Victoria pulled out her handcuffs and placed them on Zeke. She quickly went to untie Katerina. Starting with her legs and moving to her hands, she stopped when Michael walked into the room, logs for the fire in hand. She fled and hid behind the couch.

"What the hell is going on?" He said looking around and seeing Zeke, knocked out on the floor, handcuffed. "Victoria, darling, did you get loose?"

"You always did suck at tying a rope." Victoria low crawled across the room hiding behind the couch and scurrying behind the first floor bedroom wall.

"Oh, come now, Victoria, why are you hiding?" Michael

dropped the logs and walked the length of the living room. "Let's talk, Vicky. We have been partners for way too long. You can become a faerie with me."

Victoria stepped out of the room to face Michael. "There's just one thing," she said taking a few steps into the living room to face Michael. "I'm already a faerie." She rose her arm in front of her and sent a pulse of power sending Michael across the room.

Michael wobbled as he forced himself to stand up. "Naughty, naughty girl. You have been holding back on your partner." He limped toward her, swinging a right hook towards Victoria's face. She dodged and counter punched, knocking him out cold.

Victoria grabbed his cuffs and placed them on him. Then ran to Katerina. "Are you okay?"

"Yes, my child. I am okay."

Victoria called it in to the precinct after walking Katerina outside. She tried to preserve the crime scene as much as possible. When backup and CSI arrived, she walked them through the crime scene. Zeke and Michael were taken back to the precinct while Victoria stayed with CSI until they were finished. After which she took Katerina home.

Victoria walked Katerina to her door. "Be careful, my child."

"I will." She gave the woman a hug and headed back to her car.

She sat in her car awhile thinking back on what Katerina had told her in the cabin. She wondered what that meant for her. When she got home her phone rang. "Hello."

"Detective, this is the precinct. Zeke has escaped."

Legion—An Excerpt

Rena Davis

I couldn't leave Mary alone so I ran back to the party. I searched through the dining room, the kitchen, walked through the living room, the hallway of dancing students, and the patio with no luck. No Mary. I started to go upstairs, as Tristan came through the front door. Our eyes met, and I ran up the stairs.

Walking down the hallway, I kept yelling her name until I finally found her. By then Tristan was right behind me.

"I'm here," Mary said as she came out of the game room. "What's going on?"

"Hope, wait!" Tristan said, grabbing onto my arm. "Talk to me."

"No," I yelled yanking my arm from his grip. "I have nothing to say to you."

"What the hell is going on?" Mary asked.

"I think Hope saw something when she held my hand," Tristan explained.

Mary turned to me. "What did you see, Hope?"

"Why are you asking me that? I didn't see anything."

"Hope." Mary held my hands in hers. "Look at me. If you did see something, we can help you. You just have to tell us what you saw."

"Us?" I repeated, confused as to why there was an "us"

coming out of her mouth.

"Mary, leave us alone for a moment, please," Tristan said.

Mary dropped my hands and whispered in my ear, "Don't worry. You can trust Tristan," and walked away.

"What was that?" I asked. "What is going on? Who are you people?"

"We are here to help. Right now is not the time to get into it."

"Find the time," I said fuming.

"I don't know what you are, Hope."

"What I am? What I am is human and what you are is a mystery to me."

"You saw something, and from your expression, it was bad."

"I have no idea what you are talking about."

"Hope, I need you to tell me what it was. I can explain everything."

"What is there to explain? And how do you know that I saw anything?" I started to walk away, but something stopped me. "Fine, explain. You have five minutes!"

"I am a part of a group called The Legion, a group of angels with some other supernaturals thrown in from time to time. We are at every university around the world, learning and waiting to intercept any dangers that may come to the humans in our charge."

"Ha, you are funny, but seriously, if you are not going to explain, I would like to leave now."

"I am being serious."

"That can't be." I paced the hallway. "You can't be serious. Why are you telling me this?"

"I need to know what you saw. I need you to trust me. If you did see something, it worries me. With the way you ran out, it seemed pretty bad." Tristan reached for my hand and thought better of it. "I have to try to stop whatever it is that's about to happen," Tristan explained.

"Why should I trust you? You just told me some ridiculous story about angels and supernaturals."

"I have a feeling that you can tell when someone is lying. You don't get a feeling that I am lying right now, do you?"

"No, I don't." I slumped down on the floor and sat with my head in my hands. "Fine, you're right. I did see something, but it's a little fuzzy."

"Take my hand and try to see it again." He knelt down beside me.

I closed my eyes as I took hold of Tristan's hand. "Oh my god, it's going to be a massacre."

At that moment, Tristan became really serious and said, "When? Where?"

"I don't know. It's at night."

"Focus, Hope!" He tightened his hand around mine. "When will this happen?"

I held his hand in mine and closed my eyes. I was flooded with bloodied bodies. The more I focused, the more it seemed like I was there, an outsider looking in. Looking around for clues, I saw my roommate in the outfit we left the house in. I immediately pulled myself out of my head and gasped for air. "It's happening tonight!"

He picked up the phone and repeated what I had foreseen. "There's a team on the way," he said.

We went downstairs and pulled the fire alarm. Everyone scattered.

"Stay here," he said, leaving me in one of the first floor bedrooms.

I sat down on the bed, panicked and not understanding what was going on. "You're leaving me here? By myself?"

"I have to make sure the house is cleared." He cupped my face and looked deep into my eyes. "Trust me." He dropped his hand and took a slight step backwards. "I will not let anything happen to you. I can be back in an instant. Just say my name."

I sat there, a nervous wreck, waiting for him to come back. Something crashed through the window. I hit the floor and hid on the other side of the bed. Two sets of footsteps stalked around the room.

"Do you smell that, brother?" I heard a female ask.

"Yes, it is the smell of fear and something else," a male voice hissed.

The footsteps separated, one walking toward the closet and the other slowly circling the bed.

"We know you're in here, precious. We just want to talk," the female voice explained. "We already saw you through the window. We know you are in here."

I slid under the bed and held my breath just as the female moved the fabric hiding me.

"Aha!" she said, pushing back the clothes in the closet.

I felt the grip of hands around my ankles then a quick pull.

The female turned to see me in the arms of her brother. "Well, hello, precious."

Instantly, she was across the room and in my face. I closed my eyes as she caressed my right cheek with the back of her hand.

"So sweet," she said to her brother. "Virgins are always sweeter."

I closed my eyes. I thrashed, trying to get her away from me. I kicked and felt a surge of power shoot through my legs. When I opened my eyes, she was flying across the room. I have never been in a fight in my life. The power of my kick freaked me out!

"Tristan," I yelled.

Her brother tightened his hold on me and started to tilt my head to the side when Tristan arrived. He pulled out his sword, raised it, and slashed down slicing off the female's head. Blood splattered everywhere. Her brother let go of me and lunged for Tristan. Tristan spun around and the two males' swords collided. I hadn't noticed that the man came in with a sword. They exchanged blows, slicing toward each other in such fury that, at one point, it looked like they were moving in fast forward mode. There was darkness in Tristan; I could see it, but there was light in him too.

Once the body dropped to the ground, Tristan called it in. I stood there frozen like I was a thousand-year-old tree with my feet rooted into place. Dressed as firefighters, the Legion made their way into the house. It had been such a long night. All I wanted was to wake up in my room in an instant and have it all be a dream.

Once we had the all clear, Tristan walked me back to my dorm.

"Hope, are you okay?" Tristan asked in front of my room.

"No." I slid down the wall next to my door and sat crossed legged on the floor. "What the hell just happened? Do college parties usually get attacked by crazy people trying to murder kids?"

"Well, no," he said, sitting down beside me. "They weren't exactly people."

"I saw them, Tristan, they were people. Granted, strange people, but people nonetheless."

"Actually, no, they weren't." He took my hands into his and looked into my eyes like the next words might shatter me. "They were vampires."

Liza Young

"Words that can never be spoken are given birth in poetry."
Liza Young's poems have been published in *The MacGuffin*,
The Pinehurst Journal, *Cellar Roots Special Issue—Metropolyesterday
Dreams*, and the anthologies *The Space Between*, *Facets* and *A
Velvet Bridge*, and have won several writing competitions.

The Living Room

Liza Young

Here, in a room hiding behind air raid shades, an old oak rocker creaks
with the farmer's weight and space of a young girl.
A sofa, unspoiled by human sweat, births pillows with crocheted
skin, labored in the dim light of a newscast by the bent hands
of a woman who hears little more than the rhythm of a
slowing heart.
Linoleum tiles, buffed to a sheen each Sunday by dozens of
sock-footed
grandchildren, conceal tales of harsh winter mornings when
the coal
heat could not find the floor, when boys too young to
dream girls,
still playing stickball and Rover, rose each blackened
morning, pulling up socks, pinching the holes together, shoving
on boots–second hand, third, more–strode to the barn, fog
rising from their lips, to do a man's work, to pull the bales,
pull the teats, feed the pigs, feed a family.
A rug woven of rags hefts a table that may have fed a priest,
an insurance
man, or no one, reflects the years of paste wax, polished
as punishment for slacking, sassing, wanting. There are
tatted doilies
beneath ceramic Friars, pedestal jars of peppermints and lemon
drops, that pull your eyes out of dark corners where light would
be wasted.
Sunlight was never welcomed here. No colors faded, though
decades
have passed. No smell of yeast bread and bratwurst, exhaled
beer and Old Spice, ever left this room once entered.
Any heart ever held here, remains.

Terry Hojnacki

Terry Hojnacki, author of *I Can See With My Eyes Shut Tight*, is an award-winning flash fiction writer, children's book author, poet, novelist, editor, and lover of words. She is the founder and editor-in-chief of *Sterling Script: A Local Author Collection* which is one of the many ways she works to promote her writing community.

Hojnacki is a member of Detroit Working Writers, Society of Children's Book Writers and Illustrators, Rochester Writers, Shelby Writers, and founder of Tuesday Morning Writers. She is the Creative Writers Workshop facilitator at the Sterling Heights Public Library where she was named 2018 Volunteer of the Year.

Her short stories and poetry have appeared in *Sterling Script: A Local Author Collection, ARTIFEX, Pink Panther Magazine,* and *Ghostlight: The Magazine of Terror.* www.TerryHojnacki.com.

Bars On The Window

Terry Hojnacki

Red flashing lights from the ambulance illuminate the emergency entry as the rear doors fly open. A mask, helping me breathe, covers most of my face, but I catch a glimpse of the star spattered night sky and the ceiling tiles in the hallway as the medics roll my gurney into the hospital. People scurry about.

~ ~ ~

I can't remember when things changed. I can't remember when they put the bars on the window. I can't remember much at all.

In my world, every day is the same. People walk by; cars speed down the dusty street. A foggy haze settles over me.

I look out the window. Today I see the bars in the unbreakable glass.

At first glance, the ceiling tiles above my bed have a speckled pattern that looks like sand tossed across a sea of white. Given the time to stare at those seemingly random patterns, I know each tile is exactly the same turned ninety degrees from the one next to it. I've had the time to count every speck on the ceiling including the ones not originally part of the machine-pressed tiles.

Sometimes I remember I've counted them before.

I sit down at the small desk in the corner of the room. The

battery-operated clock ticks the seconds away. My notebook lay open with a pencil ready to put words on the blank page. Nothing happens. Without picking it up, I slide the wooden writing instrument across the paper, back and forth, methodically creating a mesmerizing, rolling ocean tide sound in rhythm with the tick-tock of the clock. The words are lost.

Staring at my hand, I study the lines of the veins just under the thin layer of skin, the wrinkled creases in my knuckles, and the pencil I now hold. I put lead to cotton, but instead of the story I long to tell, I sketch the window. With the bars. I drop the pencil and hear the tip snap. It skitters across the floor. Sweeping my arm over the desk, I send the notebook fluttering to join the pencil.

How many tiles line the floor of the window wall of my room? Let me count.

I leave the desk in the corner and turn my attention elsewhere. A click of the remote signals the television to make noise, sounds that will block out the silence. I stare blindly at the images until familiarity draws me in.

My captain, oh, captain. The waves rock our boat, the *West Wind.* Standing at the helm, my handsome husband stays the course. I stare at the television. The memories fade. I lay on the bed and close my eyes.

My mind drifts to nothingness. It's a peaceful place I often visit. No one knows I'm there, and it seems okay if I stay longer than I should. In the distance, I hear someone come into my room. They turn off the television and adjust my blanket so it is tucked just under my chin. Sometimes I want them to know I'm aware of them. Other times, I don't care. The quiet steps leave my room and close the door. I listen to the muffled sounds of activity and slip back to my past.

When I open my eyes, I count the bars on the window.

The Kitchen Table

Terry Hojnacki

The center of my world was right here in front of me. I sat down with my coffee and spread my arms out across the wooden table. It was here that the family came together. Good times. Chaotic times. Emotional times. Life times. The kitchen table was where we gathered. Many a birthday cake was shared at this table. Many holiday meals endured. Here is where we celebrated life, and death as sometimes happened. A bottle of Polish vodka in the middle of the table surrounded by shot glasses meant the whole family drank—toasting the life of someone dear.

I closed my eyes and could hear the children laughing and teasing as we ate our evening meal. I could see the tears of a child struggling to understand their homework. I could smell the glue used to finish the science project which, of course, was due tomorrow. I could feel the gentle touch of my daughter's hand as we mourned the loss of our beloved pet. Somehow it was different now. It would be different now. For the first time in thirty years, I took the leaf out of the table. It seemed so small and insignificant. This would be the last time I'd set this table. The children were grown up.

Initially, no one had noticed the smaller table. It took days, actually. When they finally did say something, it was simply, "The table looks really weird, Mom," and "We're sitting way too close to each other," or "Mom, we need our personal space, ya know."

I resisted the objections and left the table downsized. It would be fine.

I had to think. How many would be home for dinner tonight? Our son was going to the movies with friends, the oldest daughter had a date, and the younger one had to work. My husband, well, he might be home for dinner or he might work late. I wouldn't know until he called.

Then there was me. Always home. My life had revolved around this table just like it had revolved around my husband, my children, and my house. Unfortunately, my life had not revolved around the most important person in my life. Me. Does that sound selfish? Maybe. Everyone should have something that centers solely on them. My husband has his career. The children are finding their way. They all followed their passion. My lesson to them was, "If you follow your passion, you can be successful and happy. It's key to enjoying what you do." But what happens when your passion outgrows you? I set the table for the last time.

My favorite drink has always been a margarita. So in the middle of the table I set a bowl of sliced limes, not lemons. Next to the bowl was my long lost salt shaker, a cute, little thing in the shape of a palm tree. In the center of the table, I placed a tall, unopened bottle of tequila. It's the good stuff with the worm at the bottom of the bottle. Around this arrangement, I placed four shot glasses, one for my husband and one for each of my children. On the neck of the bottle, with a bit of gold ribbon, I hung a small note card.

At the end of the day when they walked into the kitchen, they would find the table set and my note, "I love you all, but my job is done. Celebrate."

Do You Know Me Today?

Terry Hojnacki

I backed my car into the parking space closest to the hospice wing. My apprehension grew. It happened every time.

Inhale.

Smile.

Exhale.

Mom lived here. I tried to visit with her.

Mom existed here. I saw her every day.

Today, I opened the door to the lobby and was greeted by Josie, Mom's primary caregiver for the last few months. They were opposites, Josie and Mom. Josie was a big, strong woman, Mom tiny and childlike. Their personalities, like their skin tones, contrast like night and day. Before her stroke, Mom was a kind, smart, generous lady. Not anymore.

"Good morning, Ma'am," Josie said. I heard her smile before I saw her face.

"Good morning, Josie. How's Mom today?"

Same greetings.

Same question.

"She's been quite agitated this morning."

Same answer.

"Hopefully, she still has her clothes on," I joked, though it wasn't a joke at all.

Josie laughed as she went to check the resident across the

hall.

Mom's hospital bed, set to keep her snuggled in a nest of pillows and bumper guards, represented half her world. When she wasn't safely tucked in bed, she worked hard to escape the confines of her reclining, well-padded wheelchair.

I peeked into her room.

She didn't see me.

Curled in the center of her bed with her knees to her chest, she looked more like an infant than Mom. Her good arm, free from the warm sweatshirt, hugged the crisp, bleached sheet while her hand fidgeted with a beaded ring on her activity blanket. The other hand, stiff and crooked under her chin, clutched a rolled, lavender scented washcloth.

"Hi, Mom. How are you today?" I said in my happy voice.

She didn't acknowledge me.

I leaned in close, touched her bare shoulder, and said, "Hi, Mom. Can I help you get dressed?"

No reaction.

I took her hand in mine and massaged it gently with my thumb while I worked it toward the armhole of the sweatshirt.

"He's hiding in there you know," she said.

"Who's hiding, Mom?"

Yanking her hand from mine, she screamed, "Right there!" and pointed at the blank wall.

"Really?" I said as I stuck my hand through the empty sleeve and wrapped my fingers around hers. With guidance and a tug, I pulled her arm into the sleeve. I ignored her fussing and straightened her clothes.

"They can't come in." She waved her fist toward the door. "I don't want them here."

"Okay, I won't let them in."

Her sunken eyes didn't hide the expression of disbelief.

Kneeling, I put my face nose to nose with hers. "I said I won't let them in."

Her eyelids drooped. She caressed a pink crocheted flower on her blanket.

I sat cross-legged facing her bed on a padded mat, the kind we used to tumble on in gym class. It's there to protect her should she fall and comfortable enough for me to be close to Mom while I visit. Leaning against the bed, my arms folded on the mattress, I watched her rest.

"I'm afraid," she whispered.

"What are you afraid of, Mom?" I know she probably won't answer, but it's my attempt at conversation, and I need that. I need to talk with my mom.

"I'm afraid," she cried. A tear settled in the hollow above her cheekbone.

"I know, Mom. It's okay. I'll take care of everything."

"You will?"

"I will. I promise."

She opened her eyes and scanned the room. "Where's my daughter?"

"I'm your daughter, Mom."

She looked at me for the first time today.

"It's me. Nina."

"You're so pretty."

"Thank you." Grinning, holding back the tears, I added, "I take after my Mom."

"I haven't seen my daughter in years," she said as she closed her eyes, pulled the blanket to her face, and sucked on a corner of the fabric.

As if she knew I had reached my limit, Josie came into Mom's room, "It's almost time for lunch. I'll be getting your mama out of bed soon."

"Thank you, Josie. Give me a minute to say goodbye?"

"Of course. You take your time." She patted my shoulder and was gone.

I leaned over Mom's bed and hugged her. Taking her hand in mine, I kissed it.

"I love you, Mom."

No response.

"Please say 'I love you, too.'"

Nothing.

I put my coat on to leave, squeezed her hand one more time, and felt the familiar tear escaping my control.

Still nothing.

I was at the door when I heard her say, "I love you more."

ABOUT

Sterling Script: A Local Author Collection

Like us on Facebook at
https://www.facebook.com/LocalAuthorCollection

Would you like your flash fiction, short stories, poetry, art,
or creative nonfiction considered for publication
in our next volume?
Email **localauthorcollection@gmail.com**
to be placed on our mailing list.

Submission dates and guidelines for the
2020 edition of Sterling Script
COMING SOON.

The inaugural edition of
Sterling Script: A Local Author Collection,
released in 2018,

is available on Amazon.com
and through localauthorcollection@gmail.com.

www.ingramcontent.com/pod-product-compliance
Lightning Source LLC
Chambersburg PA
CBHW020106180626
46812CB00006B/2489